THE FIRST AVANT-GARDE

THE FIRST
AVANT-GARDE
1887–1894

Sources of the modern French theatre

by John A. Henderson

Senior Lecturer in French Studies
University of Bradford

GEORGE G. HARRAP & CO. LTD
London   Toronto   Wellington   Sydney

Vouloir être de son temps
c'est déjà être dépassé
EUGÈNE IONESCO, *Notes et contre-notes*

First published in Great Britain 1971
by GEORGE G. HARRAP & CO. LTD
182–184 High Holborn, London WC1V 7AX

© *John A. Henderson* 1971

ISBN 0 245 50630 6

Composed in Monotype Garamond and printed by
Western Printing Services Ltd, Bristol
Made in Great Britain

PREFACE

THE PURPOSE of this book is to offer an alternative approach
to the problem of understanding the theatre of the twentieth
century. Literary critics have tended to classify dramatists just as
they do novelists and poets, in terms of style and language,
influences and 'schools', classical and romantic, naturalist and
symbolist, and the other convenient categories. Some broad classification of this kind is, of course, useful as a frame of reference in
which to situate Racine or Victor Hugo, or, indeed, perhaps
Montherlant; but it soon proves inadequate in the massive presence of Claudel, or when pitted against the initially disconcerting
impact of Beckett or Ionesco. The reason is that the theatre is
much more than a branch of literature and, unlike the novel or the
poem, requires more than an author. This is not to say that a play
is not a play until it is performed—there may well be unperformed
masterpieces waiting to be rediscovered, though, I suspect,
precious few—but at least the notion of performance must exist.
In the theatre of today the context of actors, producers, and companies with a recognized style and a recognized audience is an
aspect of the critic's approach which is quite as valid as the investi-
gation of literary influences and affinities. For example, our understanding of Claudel owes much to the work of Jean-Louis
Barrault, and any attempt to explain the impact of Giraudoux in
the thirties must take account of his collaboration with Louis
Jouvet.

The key notion in this aspect of modern theatre—the theatre as
stage performance, as opposed to the theatre as literature—is the
existence of what we call the avant-garde. Theatrical activity today
can be roughly divided into two streams or tendencies, the *théâtre
de boulevard*, purveying a standardized and predictable form of live
entertainment, and the *théâtre d'avant-garde*, devoted to exploring
new forms and extending the frontiers of the possible. Like most

useful generalizations, this one contains an element of over-simplification since the dividing-line between the *boulevard* and the *avant-garde* is now less clear than it was between the Wars; but the labels are familiar enough.

This was not always the case. The idea of an avant-garde in the theatre, and, indeed, the use of the word in an artistic or literary context, is of relatively recent origin. The first recognizable movement to which the term could be applied occurred in Paris around 1890, and the whole history of the 'first avant-garde' is contained within the period from 1887 to 1894. It was during these years that the French theatre was transformed and revitalized, and for the first time took on a form which is recognizably similar to that with which we are familiar today. At this point the aesthetics of the stage become just as important as the interplay of literary influences in any analysis of French drama. Both aspects are taken into account in this history of the first avant-garde movement, which paved the way for much of the more significant theatrical activity of the twentieth century.

CONTENTS

I. Towards a Definition of the Avant-garde 9

II. The State of the Regular Theatre 19

III. Naturalism, Symbolism, and Other Sources of
Inspiration 27

IV. Antoine and the Théâtre Libre 44

V. Theory and Practice of Realism 74

VI. Paul Fort and the Théâtre d'Art 90

VII. The Young Idealists: Some Theatres and
Theories 104

VIII. Mysticism, Mime, Marionettes . . . 115

IX. Non-partisan Theatres 137

X. Lugné-Poe, the Théâtre de l'Œuvre, and after 155

Index 167

I

TOWARDS A DEFINITION
OF THE AVANT-GARDE

IT IS A COMMONPLACE today to speak of an avant-garde
in many artistic and literary contexts. The widespread use of the
term in this way is, however, quite recent, and it is unlikely that it
occurred much before 1890 in French or other languages. The
major dictionaries of the French language that appeared in
the second half of the nineteenth century give no indication of the
figurative sense which is so familiar today and which designates
the most progressive elements in a particular artistic field. Littré
knew the word only in a military context, and his definition hardly
differs from that of the *Dictionnaire de l'Académie*.[1]* Pierre Larousse's
Grand Dictionnaire Universel du XIXᵉ siècle treats the reader to a
homily on military tactics, but acknowledges no figurative use.
Twentieth-century dictionaries of French, on the other hand,
admit the word *avant-garde* in an artistic context, and the most
frequent example given is *théâtre d'avant-garde*. The theatre is in
fact the field in which the expression is most frequently and most
readily used.

As early as 1864 Baudelaire, in his diaries, makes a slighting
reference to the predilection of the French for military metaphors,
and includes among these such terms as *littérature militante, les
poëtes de combat*, and *les littérateurs d'avant-garde*.[2] These expressions,
in Baudelaire's view, represent an attitude of conformism, of
discipline rather than militancy. But the first significant introduction of the military term into the language of aesthetics and literary criticism appears to coincide with the growth of the movement
in the Paris theatre, in the late 1880's and early 1890's, which is
the starting-point of much of the theatre of today. In 1890 a brief
article headed "An Avant-Garde Critic" appears in the Paris

* Reference notes and, where appropriate, translations of titles and
quotations will be found at the end of each chapter.

review *Art et Critique*. This is a notice of a book on French literature by an Italian, Vittorio Pica, entitled *All'Avanguardia, Studi
sulla litteratura contemporanea*.[3] Subsequently *avant-garde* is the term
occasionally applied to the people identified with everything new
and vital in the theatre, but such references are still few. For
example, in the review *L'Art et la Vie*, in 1893, an article on
Ibsen's *An Enemy of the People* contains an exhortation to "Mes-
sieurs les vaillants directeurs des scènes d'avant-garde du Théâtre
Libre et de l'Œuvre" (respectively Antoine and Lugné-Poe,* the
two outstanding actor-managers of the movement).[4] The following year the same writer, Antonin Bunand, writes in the same
review that the naturalist convention in the theatre is played
out, and, addressing himself to Antoine, the leading protagonist
of the naturalist style, declares that naturalism "vous a fait dévier
de la seule route que devait suivre un directeur de théâtre, indépendant et d'avant-garde".[5]

While the period of the first avant-garde, 1887 to 1894, itself
produces few examples of this kind later writers, accustomed to
the frequent use of the expression, apply it retrospectively. One
example will suffice. In his memoirs (1930) Lugné-Poe explains
how in 1889 he came to fail the examination for admission to the
Conservatoire, and adds, "Il faut dire que je passai [le concours]
dans des conditions déplorables, suspect d'avant-gardisme."[6]

The attitude to which we may apply the label of avant-gardism
has a longer history, however, than the word itself. It depends on
a concept of art which sees the creative act as the cult of originality and novelty, a process of renewal of artistic genres—or a kind
of progress—depending essentially on a rejection of the past. It is
thus a characteristically Romantic attitude. In literature it stems
from the Romantic revolt which burst upon France in the first
decades of the nineteenth century, and which, it may be argued, is
still its central force in the mid-twentieth. One facet of the multi-
form figure of the Romantic rebel is the literary and artistic ad-
venturer, forward-looking and self-asserting, whose activities are
particularly conspicuous in periods of upheaval, exploration, and

*The second part of Lugné's name is often spelled *Poë* in reference
works, though *Poe* (without the diaeresis) seems more logical, in view
of the connection with Edgar Allan Poe (see p. 155), and is the spelling
adopted by Lugné's editors in his autobiography.

literary change. L. Dubech quotes from a significant conversation to this effect with Louis Jouvet, in which it is apparent that Jouvet worked his revolution in the theatre on the basis of an implicit belief that the theatre is certain to evolve and progress, but often with little idea how and where such change might come about.[7] The same is probably true of Antoine, who founded the Théâtre Libre in 1887, or, indeed, of Vilar or Planchon in our own time. While each is associated, at a given point in time, with a certain style, their particular literary affiliations are relatively unimportant; more significant is their fundamental drive and their survival in the face of interminable material difficulties, which imply a belief in progress through exploration of the possible.

A faith in progress of this nature serves to connect the idea of avant-gardism to the eighteenth-century philosophy of the Enlightenment, which itself held the seeds of the Romantic movement as a whole. But the particular by-product of Romanticism which the avant-garde represents is just as intimately related to the disillusioned philosophies of the twentieth century. The moralist of today who makes the agonizing discovery of the shortcomings of both religion and humanism may find some spiritual comfort in an artistic activity whose aim is to exhaust all possible fields of exploration, to make its mark by a self-perpetuating revolt against a world of relative values. Avant-gardism then becomes in a sense the opposite of success, and, more particularly in the theatre, for example, an attempt to extend the limits of the possible, to surpass what has already been attained. Whereas the typical Classical writer feels his absolute to lie in the perfection of an orthodoxy the Romantic, and in this case the avant-gardist, tends to cultivate difference for its own sake. The centrifugal impetus of such an attitude produces a most complex and diverse literary pattern.

In the sense outlined above it must be seen that avant-gardism is not just another literary category, like realism or symbolism, since the label of "exploring and extending the possible" could apply to most of the major dramatists of this century, with all their diversity, and would encompass works as disparate as those of, say, Claudel, Anouilh, and Ionesco; such a definition would be too vast and too vague to be of much use. Avant-gardism is not so much a style as an attitude, and a play can be called avant-garde only in a context.

These more general definitions are illustrated particularly and significantly in a movement which transformed the theatre at the end of the last century. Here it becomes convenient to apply the general term of avant-gardism to a whole series of activities to which a great variety of people contributed. Every naïve and youthful revolt against the established conventions of the stereotyped drama of that time helped to promote the renovation of the genre as an artistically significant medium. Youthfulness and a rejection of most of the past were in some cases the only common qualities of many of the dramatists, producers, and critics associated with this upheaval. Some had little specific idea of what they wanted in the way of new drama. A writer in the review *L'Ermitage*, enthusiastically expounding a typically vague theatre project, gives as its proposed programme: "Comme œuvres: toute l'avant-garde; de l'étrange, de l'osé, du très grand (par delà les brumes)."[8] Others naturally identify the avant-garde with a particular outlook. Bunand, for example, quoted above, is clearly convinced that in 1894 future progress in the theatre no longer lies in the hands of the naturalists, whose inspiration is played out, but with the idealist reaction, still only partly formed. Adolphe Brisson, writing retrospectively in 1908, is equally critical of Antoine's brand of naturalism, and attacks the pessimism and brutality of the Théâtre Libre and what we would nowadays call its 'kitchen sink' aspect, its "parti pris de 'rosserie' (pour user d'un terme forgé tout exprès et résumant l'esprit du bataillon d'avantgarde)"[9]; but his very choice of words reveals that at one stage the naturalists *were* the avant-garde.

Consequently the many participants in this theatrical revolution, while united in their opposition to the established theatre, tend inevitably to separate into violently opposed small groups and at times to indulge in petty polemics. When an easy way to be original is to be merely outrageous, and when each faction claims that it alone represents progress, each apologist of the 'new' theatre tends to be as often occupied in demolishing his opponents as in elaborating the plans of his own group. The ephemeral periodicals of the period are particularly rich in sweeping condemnations and furious correspondence on matters of high principle. The avant-garde is by definition never static; it inclines of itself to break down into divergent tendencies. The essence of the movement is a constantly shifting pattern produced by conflicting influences.

Since the time of the pioneers of the 1880's and 1890's this movement, in which playwrights, producers, and commentators have combined to reinvigorate the theatre, has evolved into a vital element of the twentieth-century stage in which the existence of disinterested avant-garde theatres and an enlightened public encourages authors to write truly original drama. This seems obvious to the point of platitude, but in the period before the arrival of the first avant-garde disinterested theatre companies and an enlightened public simply did not exist; and in consequence, throughout much of the nineteenth century, truly original drama too was a very scarce commodity. The avant-garde, moreover, has acquired a highly respectable position in the theatre of today, a maturity and standing very different from some of the more juvenile attitudes and material limitations of its first phase. Its ideas have become not only intellectually but socially respectable, so that a professional avant-gardist like Jean Cocteau became a member of the Académie Française (and after Cocteau, Ionesco); something of the order of one in five Paris theatres offers, at least from time to time, progressive drama of merit, as opposed to mere after-dinner entertainment; and in the post-War period 'decentralization' has even taken the avant-garde into the provinces, previously the cultural 'desert' of France but where now much of the best in French theatre is to be found. In spite of its improved status, nevertheless, the character of the avant-garde remains such that, borrowing ideas and inspiration from every literary source, its mainspring is a constant, unquestioning faith in enthusiastic experiment. Whereas a particular work dates, and on internal evidence can be assigned to a particular literary school or current, it can, of course, only be characterized as avant-gardist in relation to other works of its period. It is therefore less the quality of specific plays than the atmosphere of a period marked by exuberant speculation in the theatre that is here referred to by the general term of avant-gardism. The plays produced by the first avant-garde belong to every literary tendency.

The particular moment in the theatre to which so much of present-day dramatic activity can be traced, from its most tentative beginnings to the point where it was well established, is contained within the years 1887 to 1894. The Théâtre Libre, the first and most important organism established in opposition to the conventional theatre, gave its first performances in the spring of 1887. It happens, too, that only a few weeks before the first of these experimental performances by Antoine a group of amateurs founded the previous autumn, Le Cercle des Escholiers, held its first (private) dramatic evening. This group was later to contribute significantly to the new theatrical movement.

By the end of the 1893–94 season—*i.e.*, in June 1894—the Théâtre Libre was played out, and Antoine resigned his leadership of it. At this time the Théâtre de l'Œuvre, directed by Lugné-Poe, had completed one full season and was recognized by the progressive elements of the theatre-going public as the main hope of the avant-garde. The period that followed was one of consolidation, and not until the advent of Jacques Copeau, shortly before the Great War, was there a period of such activity in the experimental theatre as occurred in the years up to 1894.

The eight years surveyed in these pages thus not only cover the life of the Théâtre Libre under Antoine and the controversial first season of the Théâtre de l'Œuvre, but also encompass the whole of the adventure of the Théâtre d'Art, started by Paul Fort when he was still a schoolboy, and include the activities of a dozen or more other theatre groups which all contributed to the transformation of the French theatre. More significantly for the history of literature, the period also sees the incidence on the theatre of the two major literary schools of the end of the nineteenth century, naturalism and symbolism. Antoine's experiments provided almost the first really successful naturalist drama; and they bore in them the seeds of the idealist reaction, in which the symbolists and decadents endeavoured to adapt their experiments in the realm of poetry to the demands of the stage. The interaction of realism and idealism is a major feature of the first avant-garde.

The new movement was never more than a marginal activity in terms of numbers of performances and audience figures, and its impact on the commercial theatre was very small. No reform was possible within the established theatre, which had fallen into a state of sterile self-perpetuation. Only very occasional performances in commercial theatres were of any interest or value for young and progressive dramatists. While the commercial theatre continued to prosper the marginal manifestations of the young reform movement, often ephemeral and invariably financially unsound, were of two kinds: performances by theatre groups and contributions to progressive reviews.

Such theatres and their associated reviews come into existence and disappear again from the theatre scene with little warning. Some may exist for a few months only; the more successful last a few years. In an article in the *Revue Encyclopédique* in 1896 Jean Jullien, one of the more accomplished authors discovered by the Théâtre Libre, surveyed some of the previous attempts to form independent theatres in the following terms:

> En 1872 une première tentative de théâtre indépendant, faite par Léon Beauvallet, avortait, et en 1874 Ballande organisait ses matinées littéraires. Ce dernier remit à la scène les meilleures œuvres de l'ancien répertoire et en joua de nouvelles: par malheur, il délaissa bientôt le genre noble pour tomber dans le mélodrame. Mlle Marie Dumas reprit en 1879 l'œuvre de Ballande et donna des pièces anciennes et des traductions . . . Comme l'entreprise eut quelques succès, les directeurs montèrent des matinées rivales dans lesquelles ils jouèrent leurs pièces du soir, et les matinées caractéristiques disparurent.[10]

Jullien goes on to explain how some of the new, independent theatres grew out of amateur dramatic societies which initially had anything but revolutionary ideas.

> Alors les cercles d'amateurs, dans lesquels de bénévoles comédiens s'escrimaient sur le répertoire, se transforment; l'on y monte des pièces inédites, la presse est convoquée et un nouveau public s'y forme. *Les Escholiers* ouvrent leur porte en 1886*; l'année suivante, du *Cercle Pigalle* naît le *Théâtre Libre*; puis, plus tard, le *Théâtre d'Art* et aussi le *Chat Noir*, qui devait rajeunir le genre dit 'parisien'. . . . Les pièces étaient neuves de conception et de facture; de plus, toutes les tentatives furent individuelles, même parmi les auteurs lancés sur la même scène: plus tard seulement se créèrent les poncifs.[10]

None of these little theatres ever constituted a serious challenge to the established theatres: even the most successful, the Théâtre Libre, did not normally give more than two or three performances of each of its programmes. Such groups, dedicated to defending

* In fact, the first performance was in 1887.

artistic values in the theatre, were further united in their poverty, their irregularity, and the precariousness of their existence.

The existence of the little reviews and magazines which promoted the development of the new theatres was often equally precarious. These reviews contain most of the source material for the history of the movement, some being closely associated with a particular theatre or literary trend, while others provide a forum for criticism and exploratory articles on the pattern of the future theatre. It is characteristic of the last decades of the nineteenth century in Paris that small reviews should have an important contribution to make to any youthful movement. The titles of reviews of the period reveal a preponderance of the words *jeune* and *libre*. The vast numbers of reviews published by literary and artistic groups indicate the significance attached to the review as a medium of discussion. Each of the innumerable *cénacles* or clubs formed by the artists and writers who moved in the café society of Paris felt the need for its own review, and the production of reviews became an important by-product of that society. One such review, *La Plume*, in its first issue, in 1889, reproduced the following advertisement, which conveys something of the atmosphere of certain elements of the theatrical avant-garde, originating in the dilettante societies of the period:

> On demande un associé ayant des goûts littéraires et artistiques pour fonder un Cénacle littéraire et artistique. Établissement comportant:
> 1⁰ Un Journal,
> 2⁰ Un Café,
> 3⁰ Une salle de théâtre,
> 4⁰ Une salle d'escrime,
> 5⁰ Une salle de tir.[11]

In the same number *La Plume* reported that a total of 1748 periodicals were being published in Paris at that time, including 56 literary magazines and 20 devoted primarily to the theatre. In fact, during the eight years which this survey covers there were at least 200 periodicals which published articles and criticisms of interest to the theatre historian. No more than about 40 of these, however, showed any significant sympathy towards the progressive elements in the theatre; these have provided most of the information on which this history of the first avant-garde is based.

Notes

1   Littré, *Dictionnaire de la Langue française*, 1863.
    "Partie d'une armée ou d'une flotte qui marche en avant."
2   C. Baudelaire, *Mon cœur mis à nu* (39–41), in *Œuvres complètes*, Éd.
    Pléiade, 1954, pp. 1218–1219.
3   *Art et Critique*, II (1890), p. 191.
    "Un Critique d'Avant-garde." Vittorio Pica, *All'Avanguardia,
    Studi sulla litteratura contemporanea* (*To the Avant-garde, Studies of
    Contemporary Literature*), Naples, Luigi Kierro, 1890.
4   *L'Art et la Vie*, III (1893), p. 84.
    "Those courageous gentlemen the managers of the avant-garde
    theatres of the Théâtre Libre and the Œuvre."
5   *L'Art et la Vie*, III (1894), p. 188.
    "has made you turn aside from the only road that an independent
    and avant-garde theatre manager should follow."
6   A. F. Lugné-Poe, *La Parade*, vol. i (*Le Sot du Tremplin*), Gallimard,
    1930, p. 138.
    "It must be said that I entered [the competition] in deplorable
    conditions, suspected of avant-gardism."
7   L. Dubech, *La Crise du Théâtre*, Librairie de France, 1928, pp.
    186 ff.
8   F. Coulon, "Le Théâtre que nous voulons", *L'Ermitage* (1894), p.
    100.
    "As for the plays: the whole of the avant-garde; something strange,
    something daring, something very great (beyond the mists)."
9   A. Brisson, *Le Théâtre*, Flammarion, 1908, p. 463.
    "its deliberate 'rosserie' [nastiness] (to use a term coined for that
    very purpose and which sums up the spirit of the avant-garde
    battalion)".
10 J. Jullien, "Le Théâtre moderne et l'influence étrangère", *La
    Revue Encyclopédique*, April 11th, 1896.
    "In 1872 a first attempt, by Léon Beauvallet, to form an indepen-
    dent theatre proved abortive, and in 1874 Ballande organized his
    literary matinées. He brought back to the stage the best works of
    the old repertoire, and performed some new ones: unfortunately
    he soon abandoned the noble style and descended into melodrama.
    Mademoiselle Marie Dumas took up the work of Ballande in 1879
    and put on old plays and translations. . . . When her enterprise met
    with some success the managers put on rival matinée perform-
    ances of the plays from their evening programmes, and the charac-
    teristic matinées disappeared."

"Then the amateur groups, in which unpaid actors sparred with the repertoire, are transformed; unpublished plays are presented, the Press are invited, and a new audience takes shape. The *Escholiers* open their doors in 1886; the following year, from the *Cercle Pigalle*, is born the *Théâtre Libre*; then, later, the *Théâtre d'Art* and the *Chat Noir*, which was to rejuvenate the so-called 'Parisian' style. . . . The plays were new in concept and in construction; moreover, each was an individual effort, even among the authors launched on the same stage; it was only later that the clichés and conventions grew up."

11 *La Plume*, I (1889), p. 18.

"Wanted, an associate with literary and artistic tastes to found a literary and artistic society. Establishment comprising:
1. A Magazine,
2. A Café,
3. A Theatre,
4. A Fencing Room,
5. A Shooting Gallery."

II

THE STATE OF THE REGULAR THEATRE

SOME ATTEMPT must be made to account for the singular mediocrity of so much of the nineteenth-century theatre. The young reformers of the new movement, who were outspoken in their condemnation of all that had gone before, may well have exaggerated their case in their enthusiasm. But it will be readily seen that they did have a case. The nineteenth century produced great novels and memorable poetry. But what has its theatre to offer to compare with a figure of the stature of Baudelaire or with the lasting qualities of Stendhal, Balzac, or Flaubert? Musset, perhaps, or the Hugo of *Hernani*; but precious little else. An abundance of nineteenth-century novels and poems are still read today, whereas very few plays of the period are still in the repertoire. By far the greater part of the drama of the last century is for all practical purposes forgotten, and rightly so.

The theatre in the nineteenth century was a reflection of the society in which it flourished. The age of immense economic expansion which followed the Industrial Revolution favoured the growth of a mercantile middle class, and this class demanded for its entertainment a theatre in which it saw an idealized picture of its own qualities, a theatre that was moral, comfortable, and thoroughly predictable—an antidote, in short, to the unseemly noise of the Romantic rebel. When a certain number of bourgeois dramatists perfected formulae for satisfying these tastes the temptation was to produce endless variations of a form that was known to please; and the development of theatrical entertainment into a fruitful commercial pursuit was equally responsible for discouraging innovation. At the end of the century the drama had not only become divorced from reality; it had lost contact with the poetry of life, with artistic values, and had become a sterile, mechanical process. The drama critic of a forward-looking review, complaining of the completely uncritical attitude of regular reviewers, sums up the situation: "Et puis ils [the critics] doivent contrarier le moins possible dans leur commerce les faiseurs de pièces digestives, pour qui le théâtre est un complément du dessert."[1] Faced with the sterility and emptiness of such a practice, the youthful instigators of the avant-garde felt the need to shock the theatre-going public out of its complacency and to scandalize bourgeois propriety, as, indeed, they and their predecessors had done in other genres ever since the Romantic revolution. This alone would justify many of the excesses and extravagances of which the new movement was guilty. The other two genres with which the Romantics and their successors were primarily concerned, poetry and the novel, were the scene of numerous literary battles and *causes célèbres*; and the opposition, in more general terms, between artist and philistine is a constant throughout the nineteenth century. Only the theatre seems to have had less than its share of attention.

There is perhaps no one reason for the depressing mediocrity of the regular theatre. But much is no doubt due to a combination of commercialization and reliance on a predominantly bourgeois audience, who saw theatrical entertainment as just another commodity, to be bought, sold, and consumed. It would be unfair to suggest that Eugène Scribe thought only in these terms, but his influence contributed to just such a condition. Scribe was the most successful and popular dramatist of the first half of the century and, throughout the period marked by the appearance of *Cromwell*, *Hernani*, and the controversies that followed, his skilful compositions, unaffected by the Romantic upheaval, were widely applauded.

In addition to several unpretentious vaudevilles Scribe wrote numerous more substantial comedies, characterized by his gift for accurate and realistic observation of social types and, more important, by his extraordinary theatrical dexterity. His skilful handling of every conceivable dramatic complication became the model for future imitators, and from him dates the ideal of "the well-made play" (*la pièce bien faite*), in which a complexity of minor devices interlock to promote a harmonious whole. Some of the principles of Scribe's dramatic output were still the major criteria of traditionalist critics at the end of the century—in particular the idea of the key scene or *scène à faire*. The opportunity of introducing this central scene, usually a confrontation of the principal

characters, was what Scribe's imitators looked for in evaluating
the dramatic possibilities of a real-life situation. The respect which
such technical precepts commanded made writers more conscious
of the structure of their plays than of their content. While this
produced innumerable mechanically excellent plays it also brought
about a gradual imposition of convention and a subsequent ex-
haustion of the genre.

Scribe's most important successors were Augier and Alexandre
Dumas junior. Émile Augier, after his unexpected and youthful
success with *La Ciguë*, in 1844, became the champion of the *école
du bon sens*. *La Ciguë*, an apologia of moral reasonableness, written
in pale and flat alexandrines, appeared only a year after the
failure of Hugo's *Les Burgraves*, and its implicit anti-Romanticism
set the tone of much that was to follow. In response partly to the
rivalry of Dumas, Augier in a second phase took to writing realist
drama and comedy of a moral tone in praise of the solid and respectable bourgeois. A common characteristic of his plays, which
became a precept towards which the reformers of the avant-garde
later showed as much hostility as to the *scène à faire*, was the *personnage sympathique*, the 'good' character with whom the audience
could identify—an indispensable feature for an audience which
expected its stage characters to be predictable. In more general
terms, one may date from Augier and his contemporaries the development of the idea of an *optique de la scène*, the principle of a
characteristically 'stage' view of life. This originated as a legitimate
stylization, but became a systematic deformation of life to suit
dramatic convention. Similar topical moral problems furnish the
material for Dumas's plays, which were just as successful as
Augier's. The moral missionary of a bourgeois society, Dumas
preaches in both prefaces and plays, sincerely believing in the
force of his message. His moralizing is, however, curiously
coloured by a sentimental Romanticism (he was the illegitimate
son of the Romantic novelist) which is especially evident in *La
Dame aux Camélias*, one of the few plays of the period still in the
repertoire. Dumas's writing is a model of drama perfectly attuned
to the demands of its audience. It is no less conventional than that
of Augier, but has more substance and more natural originality.

The long-lasting success of Victorien Sardou was based on his
very considerable qualities as a constructor of plays. Hippolyte

Parigot, in his *Théâtre d'hier* (1893), christens him the "master carpenter", and suggests that what was original in Scribe's skilfully articulated comedy, and what was genuine in the gaiety of his vaudeville, is nothing but felicitous imitation in Sardou some two generations later. His vast output was comparable to that of Scribe, and marked by the same principle of theatrical deformation. With a great command of *métier*, the adroit skill of a craftsman, Sardou produced large numbers of plays according to welltried formulae. René Doumic, in 1890 a young critic, but who was later to succeed Sarcey and Wolff as a quasi-official defender of tradition, and who could hardly be suspected of enthusiasm for the new avant-garde, wrote of him as follows:

> C'est l'inattaquable mérite de M. Sardou d'avoir renouvelé, en les perfectionnant, deux genres, qu'on pouvait croire épuisés: le vaudeville de Scribe, et le drame historique de Dumas père ... [pourtant] on hésite à lui donner une place parmi les représentants de notre littérature.[2]

One of Sardou's most successful and lastingly celebrated plays, practically the only one still performed, is *Madame Sans-Gêne*, a historical comedy of the Revolution and the Empire written in collaboration with Émile Moreau. It is typical of Sardou that this spectacular play, which in print is seen to be built on a highly complicated intrigue, composed of endless improbable details, is compelling on the stage by its skilful variations of tone and emotional impact. Nevertheless, although some of the humorous passages are still effective (mainly cynical observations about politics), the whole entertainment leaves a very pale impression, and the reactions of a modern audience go little beyond an appreciation of the play's suitability as a vehicle for the display of the principal actors. *Madame Sans-Gêne* also illustrates the ambiguity of the term *comédie* in the drama of the period. Sardou switches nimbly from farce to pathos and back again. The comic and the dramatic were both reduced to working parts of the mechanism.

While the *drame*, the *comédie*, and mixtures of these in different proportions were mass-produced in accordance with a familiar convention, a growing taste became apparent for a less demanding entertainment; and the huge success of vaudeville was accompanied by the birth of a new genre, the operetta. In the same gradual process the theatre was becoming more of a social than an artistic function. The operetta has no literary significance, unless it be a purely negative one. The vaudeville, on the other hand, is a model of the exercise in pure construction in which audiences delighted. Eugène Labiche was the undisputed master of this genre, in which no-one expects the plot to have anything significant to convey, but rather that it should serve as a framework within which the rudimentary characters are manœuvred into a variety of complicated situations from which the author has the satisfaction of extricating them. For a skilful artist this genre has infinite possibilities, and, indeed, between 1838 and his death in 1888 Labiche wrote more than a hundred vaudevilles, of which the best known survivor is his *Italian Straw Hat*. Some of his plays have more substance, however, than the average vaudeville of his numerous contemporary imitators. *Le Voyage de Monsieur Perrichon*, for instance, is more than a mere "light comedy based almost entirely on intrigue and mistaken identity", to borrow the Larousse definition. The central character that Labiche here created has in some respects an existence as real as a creation of Molière. *Perrichon* is always being played somewhere, even today, and, rather like a French equivalent of *Charley's Aunt*, is as successful as ever. The continuing vogue of parts of Labiche's work is, however, in some measure due to the discovery, from the 1920's on, and under the influence of surrealist thought, of the supposedly symbolical significance of certain situations in his plays. This is certainly more than Labiche or his audience had in mind.

The most depressing feature of the vaudeville in general, and, indeed, of practically all theatrical production of the time, is the uniformity of the subject-matter. That the question of marital infidelity, whether treated as *comédie* or as *drame*, should be so universally important is no doubt due in the first place to its being a highly relevant problem for at least certain social classes in Paris during the Second Empire and the Third Republic. But in spite of endless variations, and whether such infidelity was tragic or comic, real or suspected, adulterous or romanticized, the theme was wearing thin. Such unoriginality was a contributory cause of the revolutionary outburst of the reformers at the end of the century. But the major reason for the protests of enthusiastic young writers was the common enough one that they could not persuade the commercial theatre to put on their plays. They complained that the theatre in the 1880's was so successful as to propagate a common complacency—or, indeed, conspiracy—of manager, author, and critic, serving the demands of the bourgeois theatre-goer, who expected his *pièce digestive* to conform to a pattern which had pleased him before and which was satisfyingly predictable. Many factors contributed to this development of the theatre as an industry. By a gradual process the vast popularity of the great Romantic actors, of the stature of a Frédérick Lemaître, grew into what we call today the star system, in which the idols of the public, among whom Sarah Bernhardt was at this time outstanding, abused their power to make or mar a play by their acceptance or refusal and by their insistence on being furnished with a succession of triumphant roles. At the Conservatoire and in the national theatres the system of the jealously guarded privileges of seniority and the conservatism which was preponderant in decisions on the admission of pupils and of new actor-members were similar obstacles in the way of change. By the force of its official position the Conservatoire had gradually imposed a conventional style of acting, deriving half from the histrionics of the popular melodrama and half from a version of Classical declamation; this system was taught, and copied, in the form of the "principles of declamation". It is symptomatic too of the artificial nature of so much of the drama, as much from the point of view of writing as of playing, that a critic could quite seriously publish a number of articles analysing what he believed to be "les 36 situations dramatiques".[3]

It is easy to lay the blame for this sterile situation on the leading authors and leading critics; some commentators have suggested that the fault is entirely that of Sardou, Sarcey, and their lieutenants.[4] They were, however, only the most striking examples of a social phenomenon. The whole situation is well described in the remarks of a contemporary commentator, Auguste Ehrhard, writing as an apologist of Ibsen (who was to be one of the major influences on the new school):

> Pour ce qui est de l'art dramatique . . . un maître était nécessaire qui sauvât le théâtre d'une lamentable détresse.[5]

After referring to the unoriginal talents which are everywhere successful, and the difficulty experienced by young authors, Ehrhard continues:

> La majorité de nos critiques, incapables de rien comprendre à ce qui sort de l'ordinaire, fait preuve de la plus épaisse niaiserie dès qu'un esprit original se révèle; elle prodigue contre le malheureux les plaisanteries pesantes ou le fiel d'une froide satire. Le plus coupable, c'est encore le public. De même que les peuples n'ont que les gouvernements qu'ils méritent, de même le public n'a que les administrateurs de théâtre et les critiques qui lui conviennent. C'est lui qui est le plus responsable de la décadence du théâtre contemporain. C'est un public de ruminants qui remâche sans cesse la même nourriture.
>
> . . . C'est un public bourgeois et matérialiste qui ne veut pas qu'on lui parle au théâtre d'un idéal austère, et encore moins qu'on lui montre tout simplement la vérité.[5]

In spite of Ehrhard's evident partisan attitude, and in spite of the fact that subsequent critics of the regular theatre at the end of the nineteenth century have exaggerated its faults, making it responsible for every kind of evil, it is at least clear that in 1887 there was need for some drastic reforms.

Notes

1 J. Carrère, *La Plume*, VI (1894), p. 137.
   "And then they must do their best not to upset the trading interests of the makers of digestive plays, for whom the theatre is complementary to the dessert."

2 R. Doumic, *Le Correspondant*, quoted in *Revue des Revues* (1890), p. 333.
   "The unquestionable merit of Monsieur Sardou is that he perfected and thereby renewed two genres which might have been thought to be exhausted: the vaudeville of Scribe, and the historical drama of Dumas senior. . . . [however] one hesitates to give him a place among the representatives of our literature."

3 G. Polti, *Mercure de France*, X, March 1894 and the seven following numbers.

4 See, for example, C. Beuchat, *Histoire du Naturalisme*, Corrêa, 1949, Vol. II, p. 358.

5   A. Ehrhard, *Henrik Ibsen et le théâtre contemporain*, Lecène &
    Oudin, 1892, pp. 465–466.
    "As far as dramatic art is concerned, . . . a master was needed to
    save the theatre from its woeful straits."
    "The majority of our critics, unable to understand anything the
    least bit unusual, reveal the most dull-witted silliness as soon as
    an original mind appears; they subject the unfortunate man to
    weighty jokes or the gall of chilly satire. But most of the blame
    lies with the public. Just as peoples have only the Governments
    that they deserve, the public has only the theatre managers and
    critics that suit it. It bears the main responsibility for the deca-
    dence of the contemporary theatre. It is a public of ruminants, end-
    lessly chewing the same fodder.
    . . . It is a bourgeois and materialistic public, which does not want
    to go to the theatre to hear of an austere ideal, even less to be
    shown the simple truth."

III

NATURALISM, SYMBOLISM, AND OTHER SOURCES OF INSPIRATION

THE FIRST AVANT-GARDE, having rejected everything that the established theatre stood for, naturally sought inspiration elsewhere. In the novel, naturalism was still the order of the day, and in poetry the symbolists were beginning to assert themselves. But the avant-gardists also looked farther afield, to developments in other European languages; and, beyond literature, sought innovation in the techniques of acting and stage presentation. By making a complete break with the commercial theatre the new enthusiasts made room for a wide variety of ideas and experiments.

The Impact of Naturalism

The naturalist movement, although it was the most materially successful and popular of the reactions stemming from Romanticism, did not successfully penetrate the theatre; at least during the period when the novel was almost exclusively naturalist the theatre remained consistently artificial and unreal, and only with Antoine, the first and in many ways the most important of the reformers, did the naturalist theatre find its feet. But at this point the naturalist movement was in decline, and had long since produced its major works. There is, in fact, a gap of some twenty years between the imposition of naturalism in the novel and its advent in the theatre.

The reasons for this relative failure do not lie solely in the strength and popularity of the conventional theatre. The naturalists were anxious to capture a place in the theatre, and saw in it a field in which they could extend the influence of their theories, both social and technical, which had been hitherto propagated through the medium of the novel. But just as Balzac and Flaubert, earlier in the century, had had little success in their attempts to accommodate themselves to the requirements of the stage, Zola too was unable to impose himself as he did in the novel. One can hardly blame Sardou and his imitators for being successful. It may well be that the very essence of naturalism, often described as an analytical technique applied to the description of reality (see, for example, the quotation below from Jean Jullien), renders it unsuitable for adaptation to the theatre, which is necessarily synthetic. At any rate the leading naturalists believed that they could adapt their successful novels for the stage, and this is probably the principal source of their failure.

The process of adaptation is attacked by one of the younger generation of realist writers, Paul Bonnetain, earlier a signatory of the *manifeste des cinq*, protesting at the publication of Zola's controversial novel *La Terre*, who wrote in 1890:

> Nos aînés et nos maîtres, les grands réalistes de ces derniers 30 ans, ont pu proclamer la nécessité d'une rénovation dramatique, pressentir la fatalité de son éclosion, mais n'ont pas apporté la note neuve qu'on était en droit d'espérer.
> Ils ont découpé en tranches leurs romans les plus *chef-d'œuvreux*, et ont renoncé à récompenser la vertu au dernier acte; ils ont apporté sur la scène quelques lambeaux de réalité, mais ils n'ont pas su, ou osé, balancer les conventions, renoncer aux ficelles, mépriser l'arrangement, ni être réalistes enfin sur un autre terrain que celui de la passion sexuelle.[1]

Bonnetain admits that in the subjects the previous generation treated they accomplished a revolution in the conventional handling of the conflict of love and morality, but produced instead only a series of grotesques—every category of "women in love, girls and lovers, impassioned or hysterical; but nothing else". This ironical account of the realist drama of the first decades of the Third Republic helps to explain why audiences preferred Sardou and Dumas.

The naturalist tendency to paint life in unrelieved grey and black constituted another obstacle to any effective penetration of the entrenched and successful commercialism of a theatre world which thrived on the operetta. Jean Jullien, in the article quoted above (p. 15), dismisses Zola's impact in the following terms:

> De même, en effet, que le romanesque s'était créé une convention dans la puérilité sentimentale avec glorification des préjugés bourgeois et dénouement heureux obligatoire, de même le

naturalisme cherchait à s'en créer une dans la 'rosserie' amère avec l'abomination des bourgeois et le dénouement cruel obligatoire. Si le romanesque, dans sa fausseté, était devenu insupportable, le naturalisme, qui est analyse, se trouvait fort mal en place sur la scène, qui vit de synthèse. Le grand maître lui-même s'avouait incapable de l'y maintenir, puisque M. Zola donnait ses pièces à cuisiner à un homme de métier, et des pires, M. Busnach![2]

Jullien, an aspiring young dramatist at the time, may be supposed to have had an axe to grind. His view is supported by others, however; and René Dumesnil, in 1955, in his history of naturalism, reached much the same conclusions in the few lines he devotes to Zola's impact on the theatre:

Le drame tiré par Busnach de *L'Assommoir* est un gros mélodrame; *Les Héritiers Rabourdin* (1874) et *Le Bouton de Rose* (1878) ne sont que deux comédies, assez près de la farce. *Thérèse Raquin* était de meilleur théâtre, mais là encore disparaissaient les gradations que l'éclairage de la scène rendait impossibles. Quant aux autres drames tirés des romans de Zola, ils ne sont qu'une deuxième mouture des sujets traités et ne comptent pour rien dans son œuvre.[3]

Leaving aside the more curious examples of Zola's plays, works of a mystical and symbolist tendency which were not performed, practically all his dramatic writing consists of inferior versions of his novels. This did not, however, prevent Zola from producing a book purporting to develop the theory of *Le Naturalisme au Théâtre* (1881). The book is really no more than a reprint of a number of articles that Zola wrote as dramatic critic of different journals, and reproduces his reviews and comments of the moment with little or no modification, and consequently without any real plan. In a manner similar to that of his *Roman expérimental*, the 'theory' amounts to no more than a repeated affirmation that naturalism ought to be viable in the theatre, and repeated criticisms of the theatre in its current conventional form.

Nevertheless the idea persisted that naturalism would make an important contribution to the renovation of the drama, and the Théâtre Libre, as we shall see, not only played adaptations of Zola's works in recognition of the prestige enjoyed by him as a source of inspiration for the young realists of the avant-garde, but gave the first performance of one of Zola's own plays (*Madeleine*, written much earlier). In the same way the new theatre played both adaptations from and plays by the Goncourt brothers, even though since the noisy failure of *Henriette Maréchal*, as long before as 1865, the Goncourts had had practically no incidence on the theatre. Again, the dramatic works of the minor members of the Médan school (for neither Maupassant nor Huysmans approached the theatre) were known to exist before the period of the Théâtre Libre, but very few were performed until Antoine created that theatre. Then the participation of Zola's disciples in the Médan group, Alexis, Céard, and Hennique, furnished an important contribution to the prestige of the new movement, although some of their plays now performed had been written much earlier.

In spite of the relatively unremarkable results of the excursions into drama of the Médan group the 1880's nevertheless saw some filtering through of the naturalist influence into the theatre. Just as Zola and his colleagues were a source of inspiration to the new reformers, the plays of Henry Becque, however limited may have been their practical success, served as an encouragement to the younger realist dramatists. Becque was at some pains to dissociate himself from the naturalists, and modern commentators have tended to demonstrate how different he was from them.[4] But what is here significant is that when his plays were first produced he was looked upon as a dramatist under the influence of naturalist ideas. The tragic failure of Becque's major plays, *Les Corbeaux* in 1882 and *La Parisienne* in 1885, discouraged him from writing for the theatre for the rest of his life. The uncompromising ferocity of the manner in which "il découvrit les appétits sous des dehors innocents"[5] was too much for the average contemporary audience. But what Becque bequeathed to the young realists was precisely the genre of the *comédie rosse* which furnished one of the major sources of material of the Théâtre Libre, and which eventually grew into the stereotype that led to the decline of the same theatre and the death of naturalism in the drama. Becque was a lonely figure in his time, nevertheless; it is only in retrospect that his plays have come to occupy a worthy place in the history of realist drama.

Symbolism and the Idealist Reaction

The immense gulf existing between the bourgeois drama towards the end of the century and the markedly esoteric activity of the poets of the period is reflected in the almost total absence of poetic influence in the theatre before the arrival of the avant-garde groups. The relevance of this sector of the literary background to the development of the new movement is therefore largely confined to an influence on the theoretical views of would-be dramatic poets. Although the real impact of symbolism and associated trends in poetry dates only from the early 1890's, the period of the Théâtre d'Art, the poetic drama was not completely forgotten in the first decades of the Third Republic. Both François Coppée and Théodore de Banville enjoyed a limited vogue with their light poetic fantasies; and the wave of somewhat irrational patriotism that followed the defeat of the Franco-Prussian War favoured the equally limited success of the Romantic verse drama on the epic themes of French history, notably in the plays of Henri de Bornier. But these were academic triumphs, and can hardly have contributed to a renewal of dramatic forms. The sources of the important influence which poets subsequently exercised on the new theatres must be sought elsewhere: in other genres and in other countries.

Whereas in the late 1880's the naturalist movement was ending, and its incidence on the reformers thereby weakened, the chronology of the rise of symbolism is quite the opposite in that the dramatic ideas of the poets were so recent and so embryonic as to be of little immediate practical service to the new art theatres. Some of their theories, vague and impractical as they were, did none the less provide just as vital an inspiration to certain sections of avant-garde opinion as the naturalists had in other sections.

The most significant theoretician among the poets was Mallarmé. His pronouncements to the group of enthusiasts who met at his Tuesday gatherings no doubt exercised an important influence. A number of ideas are expressed in his *Divagations*, and although the parts of this book were only collected together by their author in 1896, many of them were published, in reviews and elsewhere, in the 1880's. His pronouncements on the theatre, as on other matters, are frequently disguised by deliberate obscurity, but in so far as there is a central idea it is that of a total expression of the poetry of the universe through a refined and harmonious combination of movement, colour, and sound. For this ideal drama the only subject is the tragedy of the poet's existence in the material world: "car il n'est point d'autre sujet que . . . l'antagonisme de rêve chez l'homme avec les fatalités à son existence départies par le malheur".[6]

Mallarmé sees the ideal theatre as a ritual function in which word and action are completed by choreography and music. His own taste for ballet is reflected in his remarks on the evocative power of harmonious movement to symbolize elementary forms, "glaive, coupe, fleur"; the dancer suggests

> par le prodige de raccourcis ou d'élans, avec une écriture corporelle ce qu'il faudrait des paragraphes en prose dialoguée autant que descriptive, pour exprimer, dans la rédaction: poème dégagé de tout appareil du scribe.[7]

Music too is not merely complementary to the action, but an essential element of the total drama.

> Chez Wagner même, . . . je ne perçois, dans l'acceptation stricte, le théâtre (sans conteste, on retrouvera plus, au point de vue dramatique, dans la Grèce ou Shakespeare), mais la vision légendaire qui suffit sous le voile des sonorités et s'y mêle; ni sa partition . . . n'est, seulement, la musique. Quelque chose de spécial et complexe résulte: aux convergences des autres arts située, issue d'eux et les gouvernant, la Fiction ou Poésie.[8]

This undoubtedly real but uncertain *quelque chose* was the effect the new idealist dramatists endeavoured to create, and, being compelled to do so by practical and material means, they naturally turned to the only source then existing which offered a theory of similar idealist inspiration combined with practical success: the works of Richard Wagner.

The key to Wagner's view of artistic creation is contained in an observation of his made in 1864, and later quoted in French by the *Revue Wagnérienne*:

> L'œuvre de l'art le plus élevé doit se mettre à la place de la vie réelle; elle doit dissoudre cette Réalité dans une illusion, grâce à laquelle ce soit la Réalité elle-même qui ne nous apparaisse plus que comme une illusion.[9]

It was in the attempt to create the ideal and universal art form that Wagner took as his subjects legendary epic stories, treated not as history but as a representation of the great human passions, of man's quest for perfection, and freed from the limitations of historical events. He sought to establish by an intuitive process a new and total form on the frontiers of music, poetry, and spectacle, in the synthesis of which lay the ideal, combining all the arts.

The achievements of Wagner, interpreted in France by Mallarmé and many others, exercised a vast influence. Certain elements of his theory and practice were taken up and developed by the poets of symbolism and the parallel esoteric movements—the *Leitmotif* was applied to dialogue, projects were formed to adapt Wagner's musical declamation to the dramatic stage, experiments were made with "verbal orchestration". Moreover, the very fact that the performances of operatic drama at Bayreuth had been so successfully built up into the ritualized cult that the young poets dreamed of for their own theatre was just as important an encouragement to the avant-garde. The Wagner controversy in France was, if not instigated, at least furthered by the *Revue Wagnérienne*, which was founded in 1885, two years after Wagner's death, and which published articles and commentaries until 1888. In May 1887 the arguments raging round Wagner's works came to the attention of a wider public on the occasion of a subscribed performance of *Lohengrin* in Paris.

Wagner was thus the god of what came to be known as the idealist reaction. In its incidence on the theatre this reaction, stemming not only from the symbolists but also from the decadents and the numerous other groups concerned more with poetry than with drama, is so complex that it is hard to see it as a homogeneous movement. Some of its members are at the same time interested in the more original aspects of the work of the young realists; and the term 'realism' itself covers such a variety of tendencies that it is here convenient, and more meaningful, to treat idealists and realists alike within the general concept of the avant-garde.

The would-be dramatists among the poets were therefore well supplied with encouragement and theoretical advice; it remained for them to translate this into practical terms. The problem was that of the evident opposition between the dramatic, which is direct and immediate, and the hermetic, the esoteric, which was a fundamental feature of the poetry of the time, based as it was on an evocative as distinct from a descriptive function of language. This problem of adaptation from one genre to another may in the last resort be insoluble. But the great appeal of the process, the temptation to which every poet was exposed, lay in the undoubted power of *envoûtement* of the mystical, the ideal, the symbolical, the power to cast a magic spell—as much upon the collective mass of a select audience as upon the isolated reader. Also, the idealist theatre furnished not simply a means of escape for its own sake, but a specific escape from the inanity of much of the popular theatre, and from the depressing clichés of much of the realist writing of the previous generation.

As it turned out, the expectations which these preparatory activities aroused were never fully realized in the avant-garde theatres. No idealist dramatist with the genius of a Wagner was thrown up in the ensuing revolution (Claudel, for whom a case might be made, was not performed until 1912). Neither was there a dramatic writer of the stature of Zola the novelist to take up the realist tradition. The real function of such sources was that, at a time when little originality could be sought in the established theatre, they provided the avant-garde with the inspiration for its development, and made available a number of possible lines of stylization in different directions which were the basis of such reforms as were eventually accomplished. Naturalism and symbolism helped above all to create an atmosphere in which the theatre could once again claim the respect and serious attention of a cultivated audience.

Common Features of the Avant-Garde

The fusion of a number of diverse elements forms the basis of the avant-garde movement, which through a variety of heterogeneous and marginal activities was to transform the shape of the theatre and produce something like the pattern we know today. Not only were idealist and realist tendencies in some cases combined—a play by Maurice Beaubourg, *L'Image*, produced at the Théâtre de l'Œuvre in 1894, was held by contemporary commentators to be particularly significant in this respect—but themes and material were borrowed from neglected Classical sources, from modern foreign authors, from exotic Oriental theatres. *Les jeunes*, the new generation of enthusiasts dedicated to the new little theatres, however divergent the writings of each individual may have been, were united in their faith in the future of the theatre. The new atmosphere in which they operated, the particular flavour of the period, was perceived in these terms by a commentator in 1894, when the movement had become established:

> Dans ces dernières années se sont créés de nombreux théâtres spéciaux, dédaigneux du verdict de la foule et des succès populaires et uniquement consacrés à la représentation d'œuvres trop spéciales, trop artistes pour être jouées devant le grand public. . . . Ces diverses tentatives ont jusqu'à présent donné d'excellents résultats, toutes étant soutenues matériellement et moralement par les esthètes, les passionnés d'art, assez nombreux à Paris pour encourager les efforts de ces théâtres aux représentations intermittentes, mais hélas! en nombre insuffisant pour assurer l'existence à un théâtre régulier qui voudrait ne jouer que des pièces artistiques.[10]

There is a note of smugness about these remarks which would dismay any present-day protagonist of the popular theatre anxious to extend his appeal to a wider audience. But the early avant-garde had, of necessity, much more limited aims.

No less important than the common aims of the writers whose plays were performed in such theatres—their spirit of youthful revolt, their appeal to a special, sophisticated audience—were the disagreements between the various groups as to the best means of reform, and the resulting polemics. The idealist apologist was liable to make claims such as this: "Le théâtre symboliste, plus moderne et d'une vérité plus haute que celle des drames réalistes, est le théâtre de l'avenir, car il est le seul à provoquer le frémissement sacré que donne l'Art divin."[11] On the other hand the realist found numerous opportunities for scornful references to the more amateurish aspects of many symbolist productions, and frequently protested at the more wilful obscurities of the idealists.

Within the eight years that constitute the first stage of the development of this movement there can be distinguished a sequence progressing from the naturalist reforms of Antoine and his authors, through the rise and fall of the poet's theatre, the

Théâtre d'Art, to the more stable idealism of the Théâtre de l'Œuvre. This sequence reproduces in concentrated form the general shift of emphasis in the literature of the last decades of the century. Both the naturalist and the idealist revolutions were necessary to the birth of the avant-garde, the one to rid the drama of the *optique théâtrale*, of sheer decoration and bravura acting for its own sake, the other to correct the excesses of dull realism and re-create dramatic poetry without mere sentimentality. The realism of the Théâtre Libre, indeed, helped to provoke the idealist reaction, and this in turn developed later into a less esoteric genre, thus deviating from the avant-garde which in its beginnings it had helped to nourish. The achievement of the avant-garde is the establishment of a young and vital dramatic movement of multiple tendencies, rather than the supremacy of one or other theatrical style.

A common feature of the marginal theatre of these first years was the preoccupation with questions of technical experiment— as is to be expected in any reform movement—and this has since been a constant of avant-garde activities. Writers borrowed technical theories from many sources, as we have seen; and equally significant for the revitalization of the dramatic form were experiments in the actual performing of plays. Acting was completely transformed, first by Antoine's naturalistic manner, then by subsequent stylizations attempted by different art theatres. Décor and costume were restored to their function as complementary parts of a performance. A new awareness of the need for a harmonious production led to original techniques in the handling of walking-on parts and in presenting group situations generally. All these questions seem so obvious to anyone familiar with the theatre today that it is hard to appreciate just how significant the reforms at the end of the last century were, and how much changes of this kind were necessary. Yet, to take the example of décor, it was still possible in 1892 for a writer to protest in a serious article that the décor should serve the ends of the play and not merely be a medium for the artists' display, and that lighting, properties, and costumes could all significantly contribute to a production.[12]

Examples like this abound in contemporary progressive reviews. The habit of writing treatises on drama and stage technique was to some extent inherited from the previous regular theatre; but in this respect many new writers, though anxious to try their own theories, were mistrustful of those who produced such treatises, just as they mistrusted the *faiseur de pièces*, and were afraid of falling into the trap of such uninspired imitation as had led to the sad spectacle of "the well-made play". An unfortunate consequence of this mistrust of mere skill was the amateurishness of many progressive groups. Such experiments as did take place, therefore, tended to further the heterogeneity which in any case resulted from the very mixed literary pedigree of the avant-garde. This state of affairs was also complicated by a wide choice of subjects and a number of foreign influences.

The new theatres, while seeking original and unknown French playwrights (who quickly answered the call in large numbers), also chose to play adaptations, of novels or of poems, plays which their authors had never thought to see performed or which were considered unplayable—Villiers de l'Isle-Adam's *Axël* is an example—or discoveries and revivals from other languages, Marlowe and Shakespeare among others. The contemporary drama of other countries was an even more fertile field of exploration. The Germans, the Russians, and the Scandinavians all provided plays or adaptations which *les jeunes* saw as so many sticks with which to beat some originality into the native drama. A growing interest in the Russian novelists is discernible in France in the 1880's, and it was furthered by a dramatized version of *Crime and Punishment* performed at the Odéon in 1888. But the real theatrical event from the point of view of Russian influence was the first performance of Tolstoy's *Powers of Darkness* by Antoine in 1889. The introduction of Gerhart Hauptmann to the French public dates only from 1893. However, the great discovery of the avant-garde was Henrik Ibsen, whose revitalizing influence was at least as great as that of Wagner—and more immediate. The Scandinavian literatures also offered the works of Björnson and Strindberg, who, like Ibsen, were first introduced into France by the little theatres. But Ibsen dwarfed the other foreign playwrights of the time. His plays were produced in varying styles by the Théâtre Libre and the Cercle des Escholiers, while *Hedda Gabler* and *A Doll's House* eventually found their way into regular theatres, and his name occupied a large part of the programme for the whole of the first season of the Théâtre de l'Œuvre. His work was sufficiently complex and strange to arouse lengthy controversy over its interpretation, and it promised an important contribution to the reform in progress. Ehrhard, in the conclusion to his book already quoted above (p. 24), apostrophizes Ibsen in these terms:

> En France, comme ailleurs, un maître était nécessaire qui sauvât le théâtre d'une lamentable détresse . . . Vous achèverez de dégoûter des productions banales et plates qui encombrent nos scènes les esprits graves qui demandent autre chose.[13]

A different source of inspiration was found in the Exposition Universelle of 1889, the great exhibition which gave Paris the Eiffel Tower. Many contemporary reviews contain accounts of the theatrical entertainments that were produced there. An exhibition on the Japanese theatre aroused interest and inspired a number of articles; a series of foreign companies performed exotic dances of many kinds; but especially important were the programmes of a theatre company from Annam (then a French protectorate). The startlingly different style of these very successful performances, based on mime, with a minimum of décor, proved the viability of an extreme stylization which the French audiences of the time would not have thought possible; and this in spite of the cultural and linguistic barrier and the complete unfamiliarity of the traditional subjects. The striking simplicity and force of this 'alienation effect' was so disconcertingly new that many of the audience saw in it only an exotic diversion; but others saw a pointer to a possible revolution in the French theatre.

The number and diversity of foreign and other influences confirm the observation that the avant-garde tends to disperse its efforts in many directions and consequently to lapse into internal polemics. This wealth of disconnected affiliations is symptomatic of an uncertain, tentative movement, but it also becomes an article of faith of the progressive writers in general, in spite of their sense of solidarity against tradition and convention. It is almost as though the avant-garde were deliberately and self-consciously heterogeneous. The two phases which may be discerned in the new movement in the first years tend to confirm the same idea. Up to 1890, roughly speaking, the new theatre groups were tentative, exploratory, and hesitant—even the Théâtre Libre led a most precarious existence, though its literary preferences were well defined. The second phase, after it had been demonstrated that a new theatre was possible, produced not any one marked school but a number of divergent tendencies. A variety of groups claimed the right to replace Zola as the supreme authority: the 'psychologists', the 'magi', the symbolists and decadents, the neorealists;[14] and as many subdivisions as there were individuals.

The phases of this development are attended too by a change in the intellectual atmosphere. Whereas in the first two or three years there is little recognition of the serious intentions of amateur groups and one frequently finds humorous references to their activities as those merely of an elegant social club—for example, in the preface by Henri Meilhac to the *Annales du Théâtre*, or Theatre Yearbook, for 1889—by the time a larger number of such groups have formed, and the Théâtre Libre has competition not only from the Théâtre d'Application but also from the Théâtre d'Art, serious notices of these independent activities begin to appear. Under the heading of *spectacles divers* the *Annales* for 1891 and 1892 acknowledge the existence of the new theatres, although they tend to be lumped together with clubs and circuses and are given a somewhat sceptical welcome:

> Depuis quelques années . . . de tous côtés des scènes nouvelles sont ouvertes sous des titres pompeux, sous des étiquettes tentatrices, avec des programmes quelquefois révolutionnaires et favorisent un débordement de pièces inédites parmi lesquelles on chercherait vainement le chef-d'œuvre inconnu qui doit être le point de départ d'une révolution théâtrale depuis longtemps annoncée. Jusqu'ici il faut reconnaître que ce messie dramatique ne s'est pas présenté.[15]

The theatrical revolution which was in fact taking place did not, it is true, transform the drama by producing one outstanding masterpiece, and it may well be that a revolution of this kind is by definition precluded from doing so. But at least the movement did bring about a situation in the theatre different in many important respects from that which existed a decade earlier.

The avant-garde theatres came into being as a result of a complex process in which the clash of naturalism and symbolism coincided with the arrival of a few exceptional personalities in the theatre (especially actor-managers) who were supported by a large number of young writers clamouring for change and for the reinvigoration of a largely exhausted medium. They descend directly from the Romantic rebel of the 1820's, and lead on by their example to the vitality and diversity of the dramatists of the twentieth century. The literary affiliations of these writers are not in general dramatic ones: in this sense there is no continuous line of influence leading from the Romantic theatre to the avant-gardists at the end of the century, but rather influences picked out from many aspects of other post-Romantic genres. The marginal activities in the theatre in these early years in no way lessened the vigour and success of the established regular theatre, although the breakaway movement of the avant-garde does mark the beginning of the tendency to divide French theatre into *théâtre de boulevard* and *théâtre d'avant-garde*. The function of the former, of providing incidental entertainment, although a perfectly valid function, does not concern us here. What is significant is the way in which, in retrospect, the avant-garde may be seen as a preparation of the medium in which dramatic writers of the present century operate. Thus Edmond Sée, in 1928, wrote that French dramatic art

> d'Antoine à Dullin, accuse une vitalité, une diversité prodigieuses, et à travers tant de formules de genres, d'écoles opposées, voire contradictoires, nous révèle un nombre considérable d'hommes de talent ou de génie.[16]

Today this might read "from Antoine to Vilar" (or Planchon; or Bourseiller; or any one of a dozen other leading producers). If, as I believe, this claim is justified, then the movement at the end of the nineteenth century can be said to have achieved much of what its instigators expected of it.

Notes

1   P. Bonnetain, *Revue d'Aujourd'hui*, II (1890), p. 409.
    "Our elders and betters, the great realists of the last 30 years, may well have proclaimed the need for a renewal of the drama and forecast the inevitability of its coming, but they did not introduce

the new note which one was entitled to expect. They sliced up their most *masterpiece'ish* novels and refrained from rewarding virtue in the last act; they brought on to the stage a few shreds of reality, but they could not, or dared not, sweep away conventions, give up string-pulling, scorn the contrived solution, or, indeed, show themselves to be realists in any context other than that of sexual passion."

2 J. Jullien, *La Revue Encyclopédique*, April 11th, 1896.
"Just as the Romantic style had made its own convention in the form of a sentimental puerility with glorification of middle-class prejudices and compulsory happy ending, in the same way naturalism tried to create one in its bitter 'nastiness' with abomination of the middle classes and compulsory cruel ending. Whereas the Romantic manner, in its falseness, had become unbearable, naturalism, which is analysis, was most uncomfortable on the stage, which lives on synthesis. The great master himself admitted that he was unable to keep it up, since Monsieur Zola handed over his plays to be served up by a craftsman of the theatre, and one of the worst at that, Monsieur Busnach!"

3 R. Dumesnil, *Le Réalisme et le Naturalisme*, Del Duca, 1955, p. 339.
"The play derived by Busnach from *L'Assommoir* is a gross melodrama; *Les Héritiers Rabourdin* (1874) and *Le Bouton de Rose* (1878) are merely two comedies, pretty near to farce. *Thérèse Raquin* was better theatre, but even there the gradations were lost since stage lighting made them impossible. As for the other plays adapted from Zola's novels, they are nothing but a re-hash of the subjects treated and add nothing to his works."

4 See especially R. Dumesnil, *Le Réalisme et le Naturalisme*, pp. 427 ff., who follows A. Arnaoutovitch, *Henry Becque*, PUF, 1927.

5 C. Beuchat, *Histoire du Naturalisme*, Corrêa, 1949, Vol. II, p. 181.
"he revealed the lusts beneath the innocent appearances".

6 S. Mallarmé, *Divagations*, Fasquelle, 1896, p. 166.
"For there is no other subject than the antagonism of the dream in man with the fates meted out to his existence by misfortune."

7 *Divagations*, p. 173.
"sword, cup, flower".
"by the prodigious effect of short cuts and leaps, with a hand-writing of the body, what it would take whole paragraphs of prose, both dialogue and description, to express, in the written-up form: a poem freed from any apparatus of the scribe."

8 *Divagations*, p. 230.
"In Wagner himself . . . I perceive not theatre, in the strict sense

(without doubt one would find more from the dramatic point of view in Greece or in Shakespeare), but the legendary vision which wells forth beneath the veil of sonorities and mingles with them; nor is his score . . . merely music. Something special and complex results: situated at the convergences of the other arts, issued from them and governing them, Fiction or Poetry."

9   "Notes sur Parsifal", *Revue Wagnérienne*, II (1886), p. 225.
"The highest work of art must put itself in the place of real life; it must dissolve this Reality in an illusion, by means of which Reality itself appears to us to be no longer anything but an illusion."

10 J. Dubois, *La Crise théâtrale*, Imprimerie de l'Art, 1894, pp. 4–5.
"In the last few years there have come into existence numerous special theatres, disdainful of the verdict of the crowd and of popular successes and devoted solely to the performance of works which are too specialized, too artistic, to be played before the public at large. . . . These various endeavours have up till now given excellent results, being sustained all of them by aesthetes and art enthusiasts, who are sufficiently numerous in Paris to encourage the efforts of these theatres with their occasional performances, but unfortunately insufficient in number to ensure the existence of a regular theatre wanting to perform nothing but artistic plays."

11 F. Coulon, *Art littéraire*, October, 1892, p. 2.
"The symbolist theatre, more modern and of a higher truth than that of realist drama, is the theatre of the future, for it is the only theatre to provoke the sacred tremor which divine Art gives."

12 A. Germain, *La Plume*, IV (1892), pp. 62–63.

13 A. Ehrhard, *Henrik Ibsen et le Théâtre contemporain*, Lecène et Oudin, 1892, pp. 465–466.
"In France, as elsewhere, a master was needed to save the theatre from its woeful straits . . . You will finish off the job of making serious people, those who are seeking something different, sick and tired of the flat, banal productions with which our stages are littered."

14 Some of the terms listed by J. Huret, *Enquête sur l'Évolution littéraire*, Charpentier, 1891.

15 E. Noël and E. Stoullig, *Les Annales du Théâtre et de la Musique*, XVII, Charpentier-Fasquelle, 1891, p. 416.
"In the last few years . . . new theatres have opened up on all sides with pompous titles, tempting labels, in some cases revolutionary programmes, and have favoured an outpouring of unpublished

plays among which one might seek in vain the unknown masterpiece which is supposed to be the starting-point of a theatrical
revolution announced some time ago. Up to now it must be admitted that this dramatic Messiah has not yet turned up."

16   E. Sée, *Le Théâtre français contemporain*, Colin, 1928, p. 2.
"from Antoine to Dullin, exhibits prodigious vitality and diversity, and through so many formulae of styles, of schools, opposing
one another or even contradictory, reveals to us a considerable
number of men of talent or of genius".

IV

ANTOINE AND THE THÉÂTRE LIBRE

THE THÉÂTRE LIBRE was the most successful and most important group in the first avant-garde. It produced as many plays as most of the other groups combined, and was the first independent theatre to win recognition as a serious rival of existing theatres. The figure of its founder, André Antoine, dominates these first years, as, indeed, the personalities of actor-managers in general tended to dominate the authors whose plays they produced. Antoine's early adventures—the way in which as a Gas Company clerk, with little more than an elementary education, he frequented theatres and dramatic societies and finally succeeded in starting his own group, in the face of every kind of difficulty—have been recounted in much detail by Antoine himself, in his memoirs, and by a number of other writers.[1] A favourite and typical anecdote tells how Antoine, in the hope of eliciting the interest of influential critics and others, tramped the streets of Paris delivering invitations by hand because he could not afford the postage.

The personality of Antoine and the theatre he formed are inseparable. The struggle to establish the Théâtre Libre has been called the Dreyfus Affair of the French theatre,[2] and Antoine himself credited with being "responsible for everything done in France from 1888 to 1914." "Action ou réaction, sa puissante initiative a tout suscité, dirigé ou infléchi. M. Antoine, c'est 30 ans de l'histoire du théâtre en France."[3] Antoine's contribution, seen in retrospect, is to have created the outlet for a great number of realist dramatists and provoked the subsequent reactions. But to this observation must be added the curious qualification that Antoine set out with no more than an uncertain determination to devote himself to the theatre, without knowing how or why. In his memoirs he describes how the scene was set, in 1887, for the revolution against outmoded forms:

La bataille déjà gagnée dans le roman par les naturalistes, dans

la peinture par les impressionnistes, dans la musique par les
wagnériens, allait se transporter au théâtre.
. . . Qui donnerait le signal? Tout bonnement le hasard.
J'allais, sans m'en douter le moins du monde, devenir l'ani-
mateur de forces que je ne soupçonnais même pas.[4]

Antoine's first literary connections were with certain of the
younger naturalists, and the development of the Theatre eventually
proved to be associated mainly with the naturalist drama. But the
initial leaning was towards eclecticism, and the Theatre welcomed
any new or neglected play. Catulle Mendès, one of the few remaining active Parnassian poets, wrote to Antoine in October
1887, after the third performance of the Théâtre Libre:

La scène où vous jouez la comédie avec vos jeunes camarades
est la consolation des vieux romantiques en même temps que
l'espoir des jeunes naturalistes. . . . En quelques soirs vous avez
fait pour l'art dramatique beaucoup plus que ne font pour lui,
en quelques années, tant d'autres directeurs; c'est peut-être de
l'inauguration de vos libres tréteaux qu'il faudra dater la
renaissance du vrai drame et de la vraie comédie, et de la farce.[5]

The first reason for the immediate success of the new Theatre
was the absence of originality in anything else then being offered
to the public, but it also provided the attraction of variety. A brief
list of the most enthusiastic members of the group at the beginning of their experiment reflects a wide range of literary allegiances: alongside Léon Hennique, a naturalist of the Médan
group, Jean Jullien, future editor of the review *Art et Critique*,
and Oscar Métenier, later one of the most notorious exploiters of
sordid realism in the Grand Guignol manner, one finds Catulle
Mendès, the journalist Émile Bergerat, and Rodolphe Darzens,
author of mystical verse plays and friend and protégé of Count
Villiers de l'Isle-Adam. It is only at a later stage that the Theatre
gradually becomes associated with a particular kind of realism
(soon christened "Théâtre Libre realism") and the critics insist on
limiting the group's functions, in spite of Antoine's protests, to
the interpretation of plays of this kind.

The subsequent history of the Theatre is in the development of
the two opposing ideas: the critics' contention that Antoine's success is strictly limited to playing naturalist drama, and Antoine's

own unwillingness to be confined to one manner. Thereafter, as long as the Theatre presented recognizably realistic plays, its success was considerable; but its excursions into other styles, in playing, for instance, Gerhart Hauptmann's *Hannele*, described as a "dream poem", were taken as the sign that the Théâtre Libre manner was exhausted, that what had started as a salutary and refreshing experiment had declined into *réalisme rosse*, and that therefore the Theatre's function was completed. This reaction was not confined to the established critics, but was found also among critics and reviewers of the avant-garde itself. Indeed, it was probably inevitable, firstly because of the limitations of Antoine himself and just as much the limitations of naturalism applied to the stage, and secondly because it is in the nature of the avant-garde that it soon tires of past glories and may fall prey to the temptation of assuming that the new is necessarily the same thing as the good. As an indication of the timing of this ebb and flow of critical acclaim, the most successful period of the Théâtre Libre is generally dated from the autumn of 1888 to the summer of 1893;[6] after one more season, more difficult materially than the others, Antoine abandoned the Théâtre Libre. When he left Paris to go on tour the remaining independent theatres had enough vitality to ensure the continuation of the avant-garde (if not of naturalism in the theatre)—a vastly different situation from that of 1887.

The first two, rather amateurish, performances given by Antoine's group, in March and May 1887, have been described in some detail by the historians of the Théâtre Libre.[1] Of the four one-act plays performed on the first evening in a tiny theatre hired from the Cercle Gaulois, before an audience which included a few critics attracted by the presence of Zola, three made no lasting impression. The evening was saved by an excellently presented version of *Jacques Damour*, a story by Zola adapted by Léon Hennique. The second evening, nearly two months later, reflects the pattern Antoine subsequently tried to adopt systematically, in that a verse comedy, *La Nuit Bergamasque*, by Émile Bergerat, then well known as a writer and journalist, was presented along with a violently realistic sketch, *En Famille*, by Oscar Métenier, one of the first of the younger generation of realist dramatists which became grouped round the Théâtre Libre.

La Nuit Bergamasque is a curious attempt by Bergerat to resur-

rect comic verse on the stage, though he adds in a preface that he
never dreamed when he wrote it of the work's being performed.
The story, derived from Boccaccio, is built round the rudimentary
and traditional characters of dramatic farce, with reminiscences of
Plautus, Ben Jonson, and Molière. The miserly cuckold, the dissi-
pated gallant, the sighing poet, and the cunning maidservant participate in a series of adventures told in humorous but awkward
verse, redeemed by a certain Gallic exuberance.

En Famille owes nothing to traditional dramatic forms, and is a
simple and vivid account of life in a working-class district of
Paris, adapted from Métenier's own short story. The author was
a police-station clerk before becoming a writer, and his intimate
knowledge of the Paris slums is put to good account. Two years
later the Theatre put on a more substantial play by Métenier on
similar lines, *La Casserole*.

This second evening was attended by all the major critics,
attracted by the articles of the few but influential reviewers who
had been present at the inaugural performance. Bergerat's influence was enough to ensure at least the presence, if not necessarily
the approval, of a number of prominent theatrical personalities.
Vitu, Sarcey, Lapommeraye, and Lemaître all devoted important
articles to the new Theatre, although it was Métenier's provoca-
tively realistic play that aroused most interest. Thus Antoine found
himself, in the summer of 1887, with a considerable reputation,
numbers of new plays brought to his attention, and great things
expected of him. How he set about shaping his plans for the first
complete season (1887–88) is best described by looking at the
periodical review which Antoine produced, entitled *Le Théâtre
Libre*.

The "*Théâtre Libre*" Review

Antoine's group was the first but not the only avant-garde
theatre to be supported by a periodical review. *Le Théâtre Libre*
appeared sporadically between 1887 and 1893, and, although presented anonymously, it was written and produced by Antoine
himself. In spite of its irregularity Antoine conceived of it as a
journal of information for all those interested in the Theatre and
its future plans. The first number was produced in the summer of
1887, and sent to a number of people from whom Antoine hoped

to gain support. It recalls the circumstances of the founding of the Théâtre Libre, the difficulties met by young authors; and the original purpose of the enterprise is at once made clear:

> Il était intéressant pour un curieux et un passionné d'art théâtral d'examiner si, en s'inspirant de l'ancienne Tour d'Auvergne et de la tentative plus récente de M. Fernand Samuel, il ne serait pas possible de donner la main et de faciliter la tâche aux jeunes.[7]

Antoine then develops the principle according to which his programmes will be selected, and which is reflected in the plays announced for the coming season: that of combining in the same evening a work by a well-known writer, to attract an interested and cultivated audience, with one or more plays by young and unknown dramatists. The question of the eclecticism of programmes, the juxtaposition of verse drama and realistic prose plays, and the eventual bias of the Theatre in favour of one style are the subject of much comment in later numbers of the *Théâtre Libre*. Meanwhile Antoine's main preoccupation is with maintaining the complete liberty of his enterprise, which after only a few months is attracting much attention. The idea of forming a new and independent theatre is not at this time a startlingly original one; the remarkable thing about the Théâtre Libre is that it succeeds in becoming more than an idea; it has a real, albeit precarious, existence. The propaganda in favour of the new Theatre goes on to explain the resources such a group needs, and Antoine describes how he rejected the possibility of looking for financial help from a patron, and of forming an amateur society supported by subscriptions, in each case on the grounds of the need to have a completely free choice in the matter of plays to be produced. The only arrangement compatible with this indispensable freedom seemed to be the system of subscribed performances or *abonnements*, by which it was eventually found possible to have an assured regular audience. The rest of the first number is taken up by a selection of Press comments, which emphasize the slender resources of this enthusiastic amateur group.

The First Season

Although from the beginning the group had been connected with and influenced by the leading naturalists—by a series of recommendations the young Antoine had even come into contact with the revered Zola—in the first season the director respected his intention of performing also the works of dramatic poets. In the event the poets' plays presented were not in general comparable in quality with the realist dramas that accompanied them. Nevertheless Antoine's subscribers were certainly given variety. Catulle Mendès followed up his enthusiastic letter quoted above (p. 45) by providing a curious one-act play described as a *tragiparade*, with music by Emmanuel Chabrier. *Le Baiser*, a verse comedy by Théodore de Banville, whose reputation as a poet had been at a standstill for many years but whose venerable figure (he was then sixty-four) added distinction to the programme, so delighted the audience with its naïve and unpretentious manner that the critics demanded that it be incorporated into the repertoire of the Comédie Française, where it was, in fact, played a few months later. As well as these figures from the past, Antoine also offered a verse comedy by Émile Moreau, later a collaborator with Sardou, a strange adaptation from a Provençal poem, and even a play, though an untypical one, by the symbolist and mystic Villiers de l'Isle-Adam. This prose sketch, *L'Évasion*, is a banal account of the remorse of an escaped convict in the house from which he intended to steal, remarkable only for the complete absence of anything by which one might suspect the astonishing imagination and evocative power of the author of *Axël* and *L'Ève future*.

However, in spite of Antoine's professed eclecticism, the realists predominated. In seven programmes the Theatre presented two adaptations of stories by the elders of the naturalist persuasion, one by Zola and one by the Goncourt brothers; a play by Alexis and another by Hennique, both minor members of the school; a whole evening by the next generation of naturalists, those who had published the manifesto attacking Zola; and the first play by each of three young writers who were to become closely identified with Théâtre Libre realism, Jullien, Ancey, and Salandri, whose names will crop up again.

Three programmes attracted particular interest, for different reasons. In February 1888 Antoine produced a French translation of Tolstoy's *The Power of Darkness*. This widely acclaimed production is often spoken of as a major landmark in the history of the French theatre. This is a big claim to make, but there is some justification for it on two grounds: that it began the important avant-garde function of importing originality from foreign sources to reinvigorate the native drama; and, more significantly, that it was the first successful presentation of a foreign play in a setting which was authentic in every possible respect. One critic at the time claimed that certain Russians present found fault with one or two details; but the audience of the Théâtre Libre were singularly impressed, and this performance is later referred to on innumerable occasions and by many commentators as the model of a realistic production. At this point realism in the theatre can be said to have arrived; but, in spite of its artistic success, the avant-garde's existence remained precarious, for the expense of such scrupulous productions as this was one of the principal causes of Antoine's financial difficulties.

The following month Antoine offered a programme calculated to arouse controversy in literary circles, since it was announced as an evening devoted to the naturalist rebels: the group of young writers who in 1887 had published the celebrated manifesto against Zola's *La Terre*, probably at Goncourt's instigation. This was typical of Antoine's knack of being involved in most of the controversial issues of his time, and is a good example of his flair for publicity; for as well as being a considerable actor and producer he was something of a showman. Many observers thought Antoine's idea a provocation to Zola, but Zola himself welcomed it. The programme itself did not strictly represent the five signatories of the manifesto: the Rosny brothers (who published their works as one person, and signed the manifesto as J.-H. Rosny) had offered no play to Antoine, nor did they do so until 1891, when an adaptation of their novel *Nell Horn* was performed at the Théâtre Libre; the remaining four members of the group contributed, however, in the company of Henri Lavedan.

The most substantial play presented at the *soirée des cinq* was *La Pelote*, by Paul Bonnetain and Lucien Descaves, the former already enjoying considerable notoriety after the moral protests against his novel *Charlot s'amuse*, the latter shortly to experience similar notoriety when official legal action was taken against his revealing book on Army life, *Sous-Offs*. *La Pelote* is a tragicomic story of a bourgeois living in more or less respectable sin and around whom revolve jealousies and intrigues. When the central character dies the hangers-on are plunged back into their former poverty. This was followed by Paul Margueritte's by then celebrated mime *Pierrot Assassin de sa Femme*, first presented at the Cercle Funambulesque. Margueritte was a signatory of the manifesto, but the play bears little relation to his naturalistic allegiances. The third work consisted of two brief sketches, bitterly ironical and pessimistic, *Les Quarts d'Heure*, by Lavedan and Gustave Guiches. From this time on, in spite of his original claim of independence, Antoine seems to be connected with every controversy in the theatre associated with naturalism.

The third 'event' of this season was the final programme, in June 1888. This included two plays by young realists, Salandri and Ancey, and yet another adaptation, Paul Alexis's stage version of *La Fin de Lucie Pellegrin*, published as a novel in 1880. Antoine was aware that this type of programme branded his theatre, and exposed it to the already considerable jealousies and animosities aroused by the naturalist factions. This he saw as the price of recognition as a serious theatre. In his diary on the day after the performance he wrote:

cette soirée est d'un accent neuf et imprévu; je le vois dans les yeux des gens où il y a de l'étonnement, et au fond, les poètes ne sont pas contents, la saison s'achève sur une offensive des naturalistes, soulignée encore par *La Fin de Lucie Pellegrin*, d'Alexis, autour de laquelle la curiosité était énorme et qui a passé sans protestations.[8]

The critical reaction touched off an offensive *against* the naturalists, however, and five days later Antoine wrote:

Le scandale sur *Lucie Pellegrin* est énorme; bien entendu, toute la presse rétrograde en prend texte pour nous accuser d'immoralité et dauber sur le naturalisme.[8]

Behind these incidents, which were really a revival of old quarrels, younger realists were producing original drama. Salandri's play in the last programme, *La Prose*, was a good example. It is the story of a shopowner's daughter who, after spending one night with the family of a poor shop assistant with whom she had intended to elope, decides to return home and accept the boredom of a life of comfort. Much of this middle-class comedy is banal

because the milieu it depicts is banal; but there are some vivid
scenes showing the 'prosaic' aspects (implied in the title) of everyday life in a working-class family.

As for the controversies of this first season, they are not simply
the result of Antoine's seeking of publicity. The extreme ferocity
of the quarrels and animosities within the naturalist camp is
characteristic of literary circles of the period; and the other main
source of dispute—namely, the attacks by orthodox critics (or, as
Antoine would have it, "the reactionary Press"; it depends on
one's point of view) who talk in terms of propriety or morality—
is a natural concomitant of avant-garde activity. The proper function of the avant-garde, to widen the frontiers of the possible both
in form and content by the process of experiment, will generally
elicit a hostile reaction from the orthodox; and in this sense
Antoine is the pioneer of the avant-garde. The danger is that the
avant-gardist will be tempted merely to shock received opinion in
order simply to *provoke* such reaction, which is not necessarily the
same thing.

The second full season (1888–89) reinforced the association of
the Théâtre Libre with dramatic realism, though again the subscribers were offered plenty of variety. The poets were represented by Catulle Mendès, with a six-act play, *La Reine Fiammette*,
written some years earlier but now performed for the first time.
This is an excessively long, Romantic verse drama in a noble
Italian setting. The critic Jules Lemaître, speaking of its tendency
to dwell on sensuality, cruelly called it "a horizontal drama of the
first order".[9] Another item from the poetic tradition was a stage
version of Edgar Allan Poe's story, *The Tell-tale Heart*, adapted
from Baudelaire's translation.

In some ways the most interesting programme was the first, in
October 1888. It opened with a tragedy by a young Pyrenean poet,
Fernand Icres (who had died only a few weeks previously). Entitled *Les Bouchers*, it is a highly coloured account of passion and
jealousy in the picturesque surroundings of a country butcher's
shop. It is ironical that this play, owing nothing to the familiar
naturalist techniques, should be memorable for the impression of
realism it left on its audience, and even more so in that it is written
in verse. The realism, however, was in the production and stage

setting. It was presented with a translation from an Italian work, *Chevalerie Rustique* (the story which also inspired Mascagni's opera), and Antoine wrote of the two plays:

Dans mon désir d'une mise en scène caractéristique, j'avais accroché, dans *Les Bouchers*, de véritables quartiers de viande qui ont fait sensation, et il y avait pour *Chevalerie Rustique*, au milieu de la place du petit village sicilien où se déroule le drame, un véritable jet d'eau qui a mis la salle en joie, je ne sais pas pourquoi.[10]

Antoine's sides of beef soon became famous, as did his innovations in acting technique. But he reflects that his audience is now different from that constituted by the first enthusiasts—the Theatre has become fashionable—and some of his spectators are attracted more by novelty than by any real sympathy with new dramatic writing. The last work in this same programme, which for once escaped the influence of the naturalist faction, was *L'Amante du Christ*, by Rudolphe Darzens, a "mystery" or "evangelical verse play"—the verse is rather free alexandrines—which with a combination of eroticism and piety tells the story of the conversion of Simon and of Mary Magdalene's love for Jesus. Darzens later edited the magazine *Théâtre Libre Illustré*, and wrote the translation of *Ghosts*, the first of Ibsen's plays seen in Paris.

But, in spite of this variety, the Théâtre Libre was more and more associated with the naturalists. The senior members of the movement were again on the bill, a play by the Goncourt brothers being followed in the next programme by an early work of Zola. Neither of these plays added much to their authors' reputation, but appeared to reinforce this association. *La Patrie en Danger* was an unperformed and, indeed, forgotten work by the Goncourt brothers (Jules had died in 1870), and Antoine's expensive production was something of a provocation to their enemies, especially since he had noisily defended the stage version of their *Germinie Lacerteux* when it was shouted down at the Odéon four months earlier, in December 1888. Antoine's flair for topicality combined with his sympathy for the naturalists involved him in violent controversies in which literary considerations tended to disappear from view in the dispute over personalities. This was no doubt why the next programme included a quite unmemorable early piece by Zola, *Madeleine*, simply to restore the balance within the naturalist camp. The season also saw one of the more interesting by-products of the naturalist approach, an historical tableau by Léon Hennique, *La Mort du Duc d'Enghien*, which illustrates the weaknesses of naturalism in a theatrical context. The play is an account of the execution of the royalist nobleman in 1804, published with a list of the sources consulted, and is more valuable as the document of an attempt to apply so-called 'scientific' naturalism to historical drama than as a living play. In a series of three tableaux, with little exposition or continuity of narrative but much authentic detail, we see successively the royalist conspiracy, the Duke's arrest, and his trial ending with his execution off-stage. In print the 'play' seems flat and lacking in structure or development; at the Théâtre Libre it was an impressive success, largely because of the simple and direct manner of Antoine's presentation.

Antoine continued to encourage younger writers, and this second full season included another play by Jean Jullien, *L'Échéance*, in the "slice of life" manner, and a more substantial comedy by Georges Ancey, *Les Inséparables*, which eclipsed the Zola play, *Madeleine*, in the same programme. The last performance of the season, in May 1889, restarted the quarrels around the nature of naturalism on the stage, and offers a good illustration of the contradictory influences under which the Théâtre Libre was evolving.

Three very different plays were presented in this last programme: *Le Comte Witold*, by a Russian count, Stanislas Rzewuski, a would-be noble and tragic affair which tells of the conflict between a countess's love for her husband and her jealousy and rage at his amorous and other exploits; the Baudelaire version of Poe's *The Tell-tale Heart*; and one of the most extreme examples of *réalisme rosse* that the Théâtre Libre ever produced, *La Casserole*. The following note was appended to the programme for the evening:

Avis important.—Le large éclectisme qui a fait représenter tour à tour, avec un égal respect de toutes les écoles littéraires, des œuvres très diverses; *La Nuit Bergamasque* comme *En Famille*, et *La Fin de Lucie Pellegrin* comme *Le Baiser*, amène le Théâtre Libre à jouer, cette fois, *La Casserole*, œuvre d'un réalisme très violent, qui met en scène un cruel tableau des bas-fonds parisiens.[11]

Métenier's play, set, like his earlier *En Famille*, in the Place Maubert in Paris, is a sordid story of intrigue and jealousy in a world of prostitutes and criminals (*casserole* is a slang term for a police spy or informer). In their own way the characters in this kind of drama have a morality as well defined as that of the conventional bourgeois. Thus the splendid indignant cry of one of the less respectable heroines of *La Casserole*, when her protector offers her stolen money: "Putain, tant qu'on voudra! . . . mais pas voleuse!"[12] Antoine, writing of the performance in his diary, ingenuously recognizes that this manner is wearing thin. The Théâtre Libre hereafter continues to seek new inspiration in a variety of other dramatic styles; but as a result of the publicity surrounding plays like Métenier's, and in spite of protests to the contrary, Antoine's Theatre is inevitably identified in the public mind with sordid realism.

In the summer of 1889 Antoine brought out the second number of his magazine *Le Théâtre Libre*. It surveys the achievements of the first two seasons and presents the projects for 1889–90. Antoine is clearly anxious to refute a number of criticisms implicit or expressed in the many reviews and notices of his Theatre that now appear. To the suggestion that the Théâtre Libre had speculated on its sudden popularity for financial gain Antoine replies with some details of his accounts, and contends that only by giving extra performances, in commercial theatres in Paris and abroad (London and Brussels), was the Theatre able to produce the eight programmes due to its subscribers in each season. A more serious criticism is that Antoine had not respected his intention of playing the works of young authors. The reply to this is a simple matter of statistics: in spite of the policy of including a play by a well-known writer, of the thirty-eight dramatists whose works had been produced so far, eighteen had never had a play performed previously, and nine others had been played only once.

The major criticism that was justifiably directed at the Théâtre Libre was, however, that of a bias in favour of naturalists. While Antoine claims to have refuted this too with statistical evidence, it is nevertheless true that he contrived to be involved in most of the current controversies over new attempts to introduce realism into drama and was associated with most of the more outrageous realist experiments that excited the animosity of public opinion.

Still he did try to widen the range of his programmes, and played among other things verse drama. In the 1889 brochure he points out that nearly a quarter of the material so far produced by the Theatre has been in verse.

> On appréciera le mouvement dramatique et littéraire provoqué par un tel débouché, si l'on songe que, dans la seule saison actuelle il a été joué quarante actes, dont dix en vers, alors que dans la même période, pas un seul acte nouveau en vers n'était représenté sur un théâtre parisien. On est donc fondé à affirmer que, loin d'être devenu le fief du naturalisme, le Théâtre Libre est aujourd'hui l'un des très rares refuges de la poésie française.[13]

The figures are sound enough; but, of course, this is a piece of special pleading, and Antoine would not seriously have contended that the Théâtre Libre was in any real sense a poets' theatre. Indeed, there was no such thing in existence until the appearance of the Théâtre d'Art a year later.

In speaking of future plans Antoine maintains that the only limitation of his eclecticism lies in the determination to provide a stage primarily for young authors. He regrets the growing vogue of the Théâtre Libre, which is a concomitant of its success but at the same time a feature liable to cause it to deviate from its original aim. He is, however, happy to note that all the plays performed at the Théâtre Libre are now being published, and hopes that a second phase will soon become apparent: instead of playing relatively old plays—often those rejected by other directors, as many have been up to now—a sufficient number of worth-while plays will now be available which have been written expressly for the new independent theatre:

> qui sait si de cette production toute chaude et toute imprégnée de vie contemporaine, ne sortiront pas les pièces réclamées par tous, dans la lassitude et l'ennui qui ont envahi le théâtre actuel?[14]

Antoine also notes the appearance of other new theatres:

> Est-il besoin de rappeler les vingt tentatives identiques écloses à Paris même, depuis deux ans, après le succès du Théâtre Libre et qui seront peut-être un jour susceptibles de fournir de nouveaux débouchés aux jeunes auteurs dramatiques?[14]

This assessment of the resources of the avant-garde in 1889 is no doubt over-optimistic. There were, indeed, a score or more such enterprises talked about, but several were never more than projects; others tended to take the form of elegant clubs whose members found amateur theatricals amusing. One example among many is the group entitled Les Joyeulx, whose activities are occasionally noticed in theatre reviews and who are content with operetta and vaudeville. Antoine nevertheless believed, quite correctly as it turned out, that in some of the more discriminating groups then being formed lie the seeds of the dramatic revival which he himself was seeking to foster.

The subsequent history of the Théâtre Libre is increasingly that of an established theatre performing plays in a recognized style. This is not to say that Antoine's group had become part of the literary or cultural establishment, for it was still a precarious existence which they led, much of the published criticism being hostile and money continuing to be the main problem. In these and other respects the Théâtre Libre is still undoubtedly part of the avant-garde, and Antoine continues to be looked upon as a pioneer. But the controversies are fewer and less fierce (perhaps because there are fewer adaptations from the senior naturalists); Antoine is soon able, in October 1890, to launch a second series of subscriptions, such that each programme is thereafter performed twice; and a fairly consistent policy emerges in the choice of repertory. The poets, with the very occasional exception of the odd *saynète* in verse as a curtain-raiser, now have to look elsewhere, and Antoine's seasons are almost wholly made up of three categories of play: adaptations of novels already known to the public; translations of foreign plays; and a wide selection of new prose drama, most of it written since the Théâtre Libre was founded and, therefore, it may be assumed, in some way influenced by the pre-existence of a theatrical avant-garde. The period from about 1889 to 1894 can be seen as a second phase in the development of the Théâtre Libre, where the interplay of influence between theatre and dramatists begins to work both ways. In so far as this second phase leads to an increasing identification with a given style, which eventually degenerated into mere convention, it even marks the beginning of the end of the Théâtre Libre, not as a worth-while theatre with a proper function to fulfil, but as an *avant-garde* theatre, which is something harder to define and yet more specific. The anatomy of this, the first avant-garde theatre, suggests that there may be an optimum life span for such organisms, which might vary within certain limits according to the individuals, and especially the director or leader, involved. Antoine, from the earliest, tentative stage, lasted eight years. Jean Vilar, as Director of the Théâtre National Populaire from 1951 to 1963, lasted twelve. It is perhaps possible to remain one of the avant-garde for longer, evolving and continuing to lead as taste and sensibility change; but it is clearly a difficult thing to achieve (even if one accepts that it is desirable) for one man in one place.

From 1889 the adaptations which appeared so frequently in the earlier programmes are less common. One of the most successful was the stage version, in February 1890, of Edmond de Goncourt's story *Les Frères Zemganno*. This was adapted by Paul Alexis and Oscar Métenier, and was notable for the authentic realism with which Antoine presented the story of the two acrobat brothers and the circus world in which they live. There is something of Edmond de Goncourt himself in Gianni, the trapeze artist, whose brother Nello, crippled in a circus accident, is never again able to take part in their trapeze act for which he had lived. But more interesting is the tendency to turn to a picturesque subject in order to maintain the interest of a story written in the realistic manner. Flat, everyday life, realistically described, quickly palls; any realist movement tends to shift in its choice of subject to something, for example, like the romantic world of the circus, here depicted. The Italian cinema of the late 1940's was a good example of the same tendency, for what started as *neo-realismo* grew into a cult of the picturesque. The other Goncourt adaptation, seen in December of the same year, was *La Fille Élisa*. This followed the more familiar pattern of nourishing the controversy surrounding naturalism and its morality: the story is that of the trial of a prostitute accused of murdering a soldier, and the play led to a heated debate in the Chamber of Deputies when the censor banned its public performance (Antoine's programmes were not 'public' in this sense, since they were given by subscription, after the manner of a theatre club).

There followed other, less memorable adaptations, including the Rosny brothers' *Nell Horn*, and even a stage version of

Balzac's *Le Père Goriot*. But these were much less influential than a second category of plays, those translated from other languages, particularly from German and Scandinavian sources. Tolstoy's *The Power of Darkness* made an impact which has already been described. Between 1890 and 1894 the Théâtre Libre audiences saw two plays by Ibsen (*Ghosts* and *The Wild Duck*), one play by a fellow-Norwegian, Björnson, two works by Gerhart Hauptmann, and Strindberg's *Miss Julie*—all of which were, of course, previously unknown to Parisian audiences. It is generally agreed that the biggest single influence was that of Ibsen, who was played in other theatres also; though there was precious little agreement when it came to deciding just what his plays signified, or where he stood in relation to the warring factions of realists, naturalists, symbolists, and others. Antoine was thus the first but not the only avant-garde actor-manager to acknowledge the value of modern foreign drama. *Ghosts*, in May 1890, was the first Ibsen play seen in Paris; but the Scandinavians quickly became something of a fashion, and in Lugné-Poe's first season at the Théâtre de l'Œuvre (1893–94) they occupied as much of the programme as works by Frenchmen. This cult of foreign drama, particularly that of Germany and Scandinavia, was nevertheless only a means; the end, as always, was to strengthen and renew the theatre by seeking originality wherever it might be found.

The most important, and by far the most numerous, category of plays in the Théâtre Libre repertory was, however, that of new prose drama in a variety of styles, most of which was the work of the young dramatists whom Antoine was determined to encourage. Three typical names among many of the period are those of Jullien, Ancey, and Salandri, each of whom had several plays performed by Antoine's company or elsewhere; and although none of them were to become major playwrights, all three were inspired by the idea of bringing a new realism to the stage. Jean Jullien's first play, *La Sérénade*, presented in 1887, is a bourgeois comedy set in a world of jewellers and other prosperous businessmen, in which the critics found a new note of humorous observation. His second, entitled *L'Échéance*, is slight in comparison with *La Sérénade*, but sufficiently disdainful of the conventional dramatic tricks to be widely misunderstood. It was no more than a 'slice of life' as banal as much of life itself, but critics claimed to see in it more than the author had intended, as the author himself complains in a preface.[15] Jullien's most successful and substantial play, *Le Maître*, was performed at the Théâtre Libre in March 1890. Described as an "étude de paysans", it is an uncompromisingly stark picture of a peasant family, though without the gratuitous sordidness of Zola's *La Terre*. This proved to be one of Antoine's most notable personal successes as an actor, in the part of the decrepit old peasant who refuses to die, even when his relatives are already counting out in anticipation their share of the inheritance. Jullien was also a prolific literary journalist and critic, and as editor of the review *Art et Critique* contributed to the public discussion of new theories of realist drama, examined in Chapter V.

Georges Ancey too was 'discovered' by Antoine, and between 1888 and 1892 four of his plays appeared on the Théâtre Libre programme. They are without exception disappointingly trivial comedies depicting middle-class life. The surprising thing is that they were all successful at the time, and in particular Ancey's third play, *L'École des Veufs*, was hailed as one of the most accomplished examples of a 'photographed' subject—the logical end, and, indeed, the death, of pure realism. In spite of its much appreciated precision and neatness of style, this ironical observation of the psychological torments of everyday characters is one of the least interesting aspects, to the mere reader, of realist drama. The favourable reception of such plays as Ancey's both by Théâtre Libre audiences and critics speaks highly for Antoine's qualities as an actor and producer.

Another typical example of the young author who might never have taken to writing drama but for the existence of the Théâtre Libre was Gaston Salandri, who had three plays performed by Antoine and two more by the group of which Lugné-Poe was a member, Les Escholiers. *La Prose* (June 1888) has already been described. *La Rançon*, Salandri's second play, was presented at the Théâtre Libre in 1891, and was considered by some reviewers at the time to be one of the best examples of the drama produced by the younger generation of realists. It is a subtle exposition of the reasoning of an irresponsible young woman: starting from the notion that her simple husband, having married her, owes it as a duty to ensure her happiness, she proceeds to justify to herself every possible whim, even spending all his money; and convinces herself that even adultery is not dishonourable. She then extracts from him this 'ransom' of indulgence which she considers her right. This, the model of the fashionably cynical comedy, although it marks an advance on Dumas's moralizing, is just as dated. Less than a month after the successful performance of *La Rançon* Salandri was again the subject of critical acclaim with Lugné-Poe's production for Les Escholiers of *Les Vieux*. This one-act comedy that turns to tragedy is essentially no more than an ingenious variation on the theme of the eternal triangle. An old man and his wife discuss the past with an equally aged friend, who turns out to have been the husband's mistress years before. The humorous possibilities of this grotesque situation, in which the old people quarrel as though they were many years younger, are cleverly exploited. Finally, in a fit of rage and as if he were playing out the drama of passion that he never knew in his youth, the old man turns on his wife and kills her, to find that by this gesture he has won the complete admiration of his mistress. The macabre twist of the ending does not, however, leave the impression of *rosserie*, gratuitous nastiness, because of the element of the ridiculous which pervades the whole situation. The *Art et Critique* reviewer gives a fair idea of the favourable reception of this unusual play:

> Un Chef-d'œuvre de psychologie minutieuse et d'émotion sûre, où dans chaque scène s'entrechoquent le rire et les larmes, le grotesque et le tragique, comme dans la vie, car Salandri, dont l'observation ironique et clairvoyante traverse toutes les conventions, *ne fait pas rosse*.[16]

Salandri had found a new note of observant parody, and his contemporaries acclaimed the originality of his play. After this success Salandri seems to have opted for more facile solutions, and the two slight plays presented in 1892, one by the Théâtre Libre and the other by Les Escholiers, add little to his reputation.

Jullien, Ancey, and Salandri were thus typical of the younger realists encouraged by Antoine. The fact that they were never more than minor dramatists, that even their better plays are now (rightly) forgotten, is of no importance. As I have already suggested, it is no part of the function of the avant-garde to produce masterpieces—at least in the conventional sense of the term.

What they did do was to contribute to the proper function of an avant-garde theatre, each in his own way, by exploring new paths.

A number of dramatic authors launched by Antoine none the less went on to enjoy successful literary careers: among them Porto-Riche and Curel, Courteline and Coolus. Georges de Porto-Riche was, in fact, *re*discovered by Antoine in 1888, having had a couple of plays performed some ten years earlier. His comedy *La Chance de Françoise* is an ironical little sketch of an innocent young wife's discovering the blacker side of her husband's character. Two years later, in 1890, Porto-Riche had a much greater success with his play *L'Infidèle*, which was eventually put on at the Théâtre d'Application after he had withdrawn it from the Théâtre Libre· *L'Infidèle* is in verse, a strange play set in Renaissance Venice, in which the heroine, suspecting her lover to be unfaithful, invents an imaginary rival, disguises herself as this rival, and is mortally wounded in a duel with her now jealous lover. Implausible as it may seem, the play was seen as a "drama of the vanity of love" and as a study of the psychology of Porto-Riche's contemporaries under cover of the Venetian disguise and the elegant verse. The author himself did nothing to discourage such an interpretation, and there may be something in it. In the self-defeating artifice of the heroine's scheme, in which she pays with her life for the satisfaction of proving that her lover has wronged her, commentators saw a criticism of the supposedly 'modern' intellectual approach to love.[17] Following the success of *L'Infidèle*, which was taken up by the commercial theatre and transferred to the Vaudeville, in 1891 Porto-Riche's official recognition was ensured by the acceptance of his *Amoureuse* at the second national theatre, the Odéon. From this point on he is no longer part of the avant-garde, but belongs to that category of authors whom the little theatres can claim to have launched, following in this way the natural evolution of many successful writers.

The same pattern can be seen in the career of François de Curel. His first play, *L'Envers d'une Sainte*, was presented at the Théâtre Libre in February 1892. This is a skilfully handled account of the past life and the psychological development of a woman who, at the beginning of the play, arrives home from years of seclusion in a convent and at the end returns to her seclusion, having discovered that there is no longer any place for her in the outside world. Eighteen years earlier Julie Renaudin had become a nun in an act of proud self-sacrifice on discovering that her childhood idol, Henri, was to marry another person. This fact and the complex of relationships grown round it—notably between the daughter of this marriage and some of Julie's young lady pupils in her convent school—are gradually revealed, through the presence of Henri's widow and in spite of the benign incomprehension of Julie's mother. The decision to return to the convent and to a position of respect there is not only dramatically satisfying but psychologically convincing. Curel had, in fact, produced a valid and serious play which did not need to demonstrate a truth or prove a thesis, since it existed for its own sake. In November of the same year Antoine reinforced Curel's success by presenting his second play, *Les Fossiles,* which led to his recognition as a dramatist of considerable qualities. It paints the picture of an aristocratic family out of touch with the modern world and tied to traditional values. Everything, for these fossils of the nobility, is subordinated to preserving the ducal name through a male heir. The heir in question turns out to be the illegitimate child of a servant-companion in the household, who has been the mistress not only of the son of the house, to whom she is eventually married, but also of his father the Duke. The son, dying of consumption and aware that the child's parentage is in doubt, nevertheless appeals in his will to the surviving members of the family, all of whom have been hurt in some way by these events, to devote themselves to the upbringing of the young heir in order that the noble name may not die out. Personal pride is gloriously sacrificed to aristocratic values, however wrong-headed. After *Les Fossiles* Curel used the less revolutionary Théâtre d'Application (just as Porto-Riche had done) as a stepping-stone to acceptance on the regular stage. His third play, a mediocre comedy, was performed there prior to its presentation at the Vaudeville, and a few months later *L'Amour brode*, a much more substantial play, was given at the Comédie Française. Curel pursued a successful career as a dramatist further than most, and even became a member of the Académie Française. This is simply an extreme example of what seems to be a natural progression: from left wing to right, youth to old age, radical to reactionary.

Georges Courteline and Romain Coolus, both successful

humorists, also owe their first success to Antoine. Coolus's first play, *Le Ménage Brésile*, is a slight comedy, but brings a welcome note of irony to the eternal subject of *cocuage*: Brésile, a comfortable bourgeois, receives the three hundred and twenty-fourth letter informing him that his wife is deceiving him, and intimates that he finds the whole business an excellent joke. Three months later, in April 1893, Antoine gave *Boubouroche*, by Georges Courteline. This was Courteline's second play, and remains his best-known work. His only two-act play, *Boubouroche* is a picture of a farcical character whose benign innocence is such that he is the easy victim of the most monstrous deceptions. Its first performance was an enormous success and received almost universal critical approval—a most exceptional occurrence at the Théâtre Libre.

Some of the new drama of less obvious merit might not have attracted Antoine's attention, one suspects, had it not been for its publicity value. Such was, for example, *Le Père Lebonnard*, by Jean Aicard, who, like Curel but with perhaps less justification, was to join the 'immortal' ranks of the Académie. His play opened Antoine's 1889–90 season, having been refused—after rehearsals —at the Comédie Française. It is a verse drama based on a suspiciously neat plot of family complications which are all straightened out for the final curtain, and was accompanied by a curtain-raiser which Aicard wrote for the Théâtre Libre presentation, *Dans le Guignol*, which is merely a lampoon of the *sociétaires* of the members' committee at the Comédie Française who had refused his play. Pierre Wolff's first play was included in the Théâtre Libre programme of May 1890 for similar reasons. The play itself, *Jacques Bouchard*, is a slight *comédie rosse* which Antoine considered one of the most violent plays he had produced. But the real point was that the author was the nephew of the eminent traditionalist critic Albert Wolff, who left the Theatre in a violent rage after seeing the play. Pierre Wolff's later plays at the Théâtre Libre are quite unmemorable, but he subsequently enjoyed great popular success in the commercial theatre. The same season that saw Wolff's first play also included, a month later, a drama which caused great excitement: with the provocative title of *Les Chapons*, it depicted the faint-hearted reactions of a bourgeois French family during the Prussian occupation of 1870–71. This was apparently too fresh in the minds of some members of the audience to constitute an acceptable subject if presented in anything but the most patriotic terms, and the play even led to fighting in the Theatre. *Les Chapons* was adapted by Lucien Descaves and Georges Darien from a novel by the former.

There is one other type of play seen at the Théâtre Libre and elsewhere which is worth a mention: the play of political and social comment. The first of this kind, in February 1891, was *La Meule*, by Georges Lecomte, presented by Antoine. *La Meule* is the story of an honest man made the dupe of a dishonest society and grown alternately weak and cynical through contact with the corrupting influence of money. A similar subject was taken up by Eugène Brieux in his play *L'Engrenage*. Brieux, like Lecomte yet another future *académicien* and successful dramatist, had already had two full-length plays performed at the Théâtre Libre, the first, *Ménage d'Artistes*, containing an interesting study of the artist's mentality and a satirical picture of the world of critics. *L'Engrenage* was given, however, to Les Escholiers, where it was performed in May 1894, after Antoine had shown preference to a similar political drama by Maurice Barrès, *Une Journée Parlementaire*. *L'Engrenage* gives a good picture of the world of politics, and its pessimistic conclusion is that the dishonest man always wins.

Rémoussin, a provincial businessman, is persuaded to enter parliament and does so with the best intentions. From the moment he agrees to become a candidate the gradual and inevitable process of corruption and compromise gains ground, his friends and relations conspire to increase his influence, and finally he accepts a considerable bribe "because everyone else does . . ." This is offered in connection with the financing of a tunnel under the Alps, but is in fact a thinly disguised allusion to the scandal of the Panama Canal shares, in which many deputies had been implicated. Rémoussin's mistake is inevitable: "Parce que ça c'est un engrenage et une fois qu'on y a mis le doigt, on ne peut faire autrement que d'y passer tout entier."[18] When it seems that the affair is to be made public Rémoussin, in an attempt to regain his self-respect, writes a letter of confession; only to find that so many important people were implicated that the scandal is hushed up, and therefore that Rémoussin himself is the only guilty politician whose name is published. He is ruined, and his dishonest colleague triumphs.

A subject of this nature provided a field where simple realism was still entirely acceptable, in that the literary function was reduced to the most direct and forceful expression of the situation. Such was the provocative topicality of *L'Engrenage* that it had been banned by the censor, though this ban did not apply to private groups like Les Escholiers, curiously enough, even when they played before an invited audience including regular critics. Antoine had rejected *L'Engrenage*, or, rather, had preferred Barrès's play on a similar theme. This choice was made by Antoine, at the risk of antagonizing Brieux, for the quite unartistic reason that the notoriety of Barrès was sure to attract considerable attention. It is also true that whereas Barrès had had nothing performed previously, Brieux had already given two plays at the Théâtre Libre. Barrès's *Une Journée Parlementaire*, played at the Théâtre Libre in February 1894, is an exposure of the intrigues behind the parliamentary scene. The author's only excursion into drama, it centres round the dishonest politician Thuringe, who, after unscrupulous attempts to buy off journalist enemies who have information against him, is manœuvred into a position from which the only escape is suicide. The best parts of this play are scenes in the lobbies of the Palais-Bourbon.

To measure the success of the Théâtre Libre one must first determine what it set out to achieve. This is by no means obvious, if one recalls Antoine's description, quoted at the start of this chapter, of the way in which the whole thing began. In its initial purpose of providing a stage for young authors the Théâtre Libre was clearly a success, though its professed eclecticism was not—indeed, to maintain a truly eclectic approach may well be impossible. Antoine's diary again reveals how his ideas changed (this is an entry dated January 1891):

Un comité de poètes s'est formé pour créer un Théâtre d'Art qui donnera bientôt . . . des pièces de Pierre Quillard, Rachilde et Stéphane Mallarmé. C'est fort bien, car le Théâtre Libre ne suffit plus, d'autres groupements deviennent nécessaires pour jouer certaines œuvres que nous ne pouvons pas réaliser chez nous. Je n'y vois pas une concurrence, mais un complément dans l'évolution qui s'accélère.[19]

At its height the Théâtre Libre provided a real stimulus to young dramatists, and in the May 1890 number of the *Théâtre Libre* magazine Antoine gave elaborate details of his plans for building a new public theatre to which he hoped his company would move, and which would follow his policy of performing unknown dramatists. For financial reasons these enthusiastic plans failed to mature; and the lengthy descriptions in this number, with architect's drawings and administrative details, were never more than a project on paper, a vision of what might have been. For two seasons Rodolphe Darzens produced a different magazine, entitled *Le Théâtre Libre Illustré*, which appeared on the occasion of each performance with informative articles about the programme; but this ceased to appear in the summer of 1891. The Théâtre Libre never succeeded in becoming a regular, established theatre, and was never financially viable.

But at least its existence, and influence, was officially recognized. In December 1890 in the course of a parliamentary debate a Senator protested that the Government was subsidizing the Théâtre Libre, in that the Ministre des Beaux-Arts had officially subscribed to four *abonnements* for Antoine's monthly performance. This was, in fact, a dubious compliment, as tickets were thereby available for official visitors, concerned among other things with the possible censorship of plays which might come to be performed in public. This debate also led to the expression in parliament of a variety of hostile or sympathetic opinions.

At the end of the penultimate season, in the summer of 1893, Antoine's diary begins to show that the glorious experiment of the Théâtre Libre may be coming to an end. He describes the desperate financial situation, and sums up recent progress thus:

> A vrai dire, je sens bien aussi au point de vue artistique, que nous arrivons au bout du rouleau et que notre mouvement touche à sa fin. Depuis deux ans, il m'a fallu appeler à la rescousse le théâtre étranger, les curiosités sensationnelles pour meubler les intervalles de nos véritables manifestations, mais tout cela s'épuise. La saison n'a vraiment apporté que *Boubouroche* et l'immense retentissement des *Tisserands* n'est en somme qu'une répétition de Tolstoï ou d'Ibsen.[20]

Gerhart Hauptmann's *The Weavers* was, in fact, one of the great discoveries of the year, and this no doubt prompted Antoine to produce a very different Hauptmann play, *L'Assomption de Hannele Mattern* (*Hanneles Himmelfahrt*) in February 1894. This "dream poem" was possibly too far removed from the normal Théâtre Libre style to be properly understood there, or even perhaps to be adequately handled by the realist Antoine. The rest of the last season (1893–94), which consisted of only five programmes and was beset with financial difficulties, included one other foreign play, *Une Faillite*, by the Norwegian Björnson, and also the Barrès play, *Une Journée Parlementaire*, described above. The very last work which Antoine produced at the Théâtre Libre, in April 1894, was a curious hybrid described by its author, Marcel Luguet, as a "theatrical novel". Entitled *Le Missionnaire* it tells of an idealized and idealistic young woman, who is driven to suicide as a result of a sudden contact with harsh reality. It is written half in dramatic dialogue and half in continuous narrative prose. The narrative was read by Antoine on stage, in the manner of a chorus. He notes how it was the unfavourable reception of this play that finally persuaded him to abandon his debt-ridden Theatre: as he sat reading the part of the narrator a handful of small change was thrown on to the stage.

A few days later he announced that he was postponing the three programmes still owing to his subscribers, and set off with his company on tour abroad. The last three *spectacles* were finally given, by his assistant Larochelle, in the first months of 1895. The fiasco of this last season demonstrated not only that the Théâtre Libre manner was played out, but also that the prestige of naturalism, on which the Theatre's reputation had been largely built, was a thing of the past as far as the drama was concerned. It is worth recalling, however, that the Théâtre Libre reached its climax more than a decade after the success of naturalism in the novel, and that while the Theatre played a number of works of the older naturalists which had until then been considered as nothing but glorious failures, it also proved invaluable as an outlet for the younger generation of realists (since one can hardly describe such a diverse group by a more precise term). Apart from the recognized success of Curel, Porto-Riche, Coolus and Courteline, and Eugène Brieux—consolidated in regular theatres—the Théâtre Libre gave the initial impulse to the literary career of numerous minor figures, not all of whom continued to write for the stage. It could even boast of having launched five future members of the Académie Française—Curel, Brieux, Barrès, Aicard, and Lecomte —though whether this is much of a claim to fame is arguable, to say the least. Pierre Wolff, mentioned above (p. 64), was one who became a highly successful dramatist of the *théâtre de boulevard*. Others were more active as critics and commentators (Paul Ginisty, Jean Jullien) or as novelists (Henri Fèvre, Georges Lecomte). Oscar Métenier continued to write short plays with a tendency towards the horrific, and in 1896 founded his own theatre in which to play them, the Grand Guignol, which continued for many years to play a debased form of the *genre rosse*. After their success at the Théâtre Libre neither Georges Ancey nor Gaston Salandri produced much of interest.

In spite of the rise of this generation of young realists grouped round the Théâtre Libre the overall impression of its programmes is one of surprising variety. This is perhaps attributable to Antoine's willingness to perform any kind of work, regardless of the suitability of the troupe or the theatre at his disposal. A refusal to be limited by mere practical considerations is characteristic of him, and in some ways offers a pattern for future avant-gardists. The immense revolution accomplished or set in motion by Antoine as an actor and producer also had its effect on the later evolution of the avant-garde. It is, of course, difficult, at this distance in time, to appreciate what Antoine did for acting, but some of his views are recorded in a letter, reprinted in the *Théâtre Libre* (an undated number, which appeared in late 1893). The letter discusses the problems of the actor and his relationship to the dramatist, and is addressed to Le Bargy, a young actor-member of the Comédie Française. Le Bargy, having been cast in an important part in Curel's latest play, felt that the character he was to play was "not sufficiently sympathetic", and discreetly suggested that some alterations should be made to the text. This provides Antoine with an opportunity to launch a violent attack against such practices, against the unsubtle minds of established actors, and against anything tending to interfere with the author's sole responsibility for his play:

Je voudrais tenter de vous convaincre . . . que les comédiens ne connaissent jamais rien aux pièces qu'ils doivent jouer. Leur métier est de les jouer tout bonnement, d'interpréter le mieux

possible des personnages dont la conception leur échappe. . . .
L'écart intellectuel entre le poète et son interprète est si infran-
chissable, que jamais celui-ci ne satisfait complètement le
premier.[21]

Antoine concludes with an appeal to Le Bargy and his young
colleagues to join the battle on the side of the revolutionary movement of young dramatists and actors anxious to do away with out-
dated conventions. To see this in perspective one should remember
that for every Antoine there were a dozen Le Bargys. Antoine's
silences, his sides of beef, his back resolutely turned to the audience, all became symbols of the revolution which he started,
symbols of a new freedom, the freedom to create, which was put
to such remarkable use by his successors, the theatrical giants of
the inter-War period, Copeau and the *cartel des quatre*.

The most remarkable feature of the Théâtre Libre is that it
managed to survive as long as it did. In the course of producing
over a hundred new plays in seven years the Théâtre Libre
aroused such enmity and jealousy as only success can inspire.
Thus Antoine's group was the first to prove that an avant-garde
theatre was possible. By the time it reached its decline, although
Antoine makes little mention of them, a number of other groups
were functioning, and to some extent taking the place of the
Théâtre Libre. Some, like Antoine, had leanings towards realism;
others became the mouthpieces of literary schools which Antoine
and his supporters were unwilling or unable to serve.

Notes

1   A. Antoine, *"Mes Souvenirs" sur le Théâtre Libre*, Fayard, 1921.
    Also A. Thalasso, *Le Théâtre Libre*, Mercure de France, 1909;
    S. M. Waxman, *Antoine and the Théâtre Libre*, Harvard, 1926;
    M. Roussou, *André Antoine*, Éditions de l'Arche, 1956.
2   J.-R. Bloch, *Destin du Théâtre*, Gallimard, 1930.
3   L. Dubech, *La Crise du Théâtre*, Librairie de France, 1928.
    "Action or reaction, his powerful effort instigated, directed, or
    inflected everything. Monsieur Antoine is thirty years of the
    history of the theatre in France."

4 "*Mes Souvenirs*", p. 9. This book is an edited version of Antoine's diary, and contains detail on almost every Théâtre Libre performance.

"The battle which was already won in the novel by the naturalists, in painting by the impressionists, in music by the Wagnerians, was about to move into the theatre.

. . . Who was to give the signal? Quite simply, chance. Without being aware of it in the least, I was to become the animator of forces which I did not even suspect."

5 Quoted by Antoine, "*Mes Souvenirs*", p. 69.

"The stage on which you are performing plays with your young friends is the consolation of old Romantics at the same time as the hope of the young naturalists. . . . In a few evenings you have done much more for dramatic art than so many other managers in years; perhaps it will be from the inauguration of your free stage that we shall have to date the rebirth of real drama, real comedy and farce."

6 See, for example, Thalasso, p. 70.

7 *Le Théâtre Libre*, I (1887), p. 4.

"It was interesting for someone who was both curious and enthusiastic about the theatre to see whether it would not be possible, taking one's inspiration from the old Tour d'Auvergne and from Monsieur Fernand Samuel's more recent effort, to give the young a hand and make things easier for them."

Samuel, in 1887 director of a commercial theatre, had started the abortive project some ten years earlier of a "Cercle des Arts intimes".

8 Antoine, "*Mes Souvenirs*", pp. 103, 104.

"this evening strikes a new and unexpected note; I see it in the astonishment in people's eyes, and, really, the poets are unhappy, the season is finishing on an offensive by the naturalists, emphasized by *La Fin de Lucie Pellegrin*, by Alexis, which was surrounded by tremendous curiosity and which went off without protest."

"The scandal about *Lucie Pellegrin* is enormous; of course, all the reactionary Press is using it as an excuse to accuse us of immorality and speak ill of naturalism."

9 "Un drame horizontal de grande marque", quoted by Edmond Sée, *Le Théâtre français contemporain*, Colin, 1928, p. 124.

10 Antoine, "*Mes Souvenirs*", p. 117.

"So as to get the stage setting just right, for *The Butchers* I had hung up real sides of meat, which had a sensational effect, and for *Cavalleria Rusticana*, in the middle of the square of the little

Sicilian village where the play takes place, there was a real foun-
tain, which delighted the audience, I don't know why."

11   Quoted by Thalasso, *Le Théâtre Libre*, pp. 229–230.
"*Important notice*: The wide-ranging eclecticism which has led us,
with an equal respect for all literary schools, to perform the most
varied works, *La Nuit Bergamasque* and *En Famille*, *La Fin de Lucie
Pellegrin* and *Le Baiser*, now brings the Théâtre Libre to play *La
Casserole*, a work of very violent realism, which paints a cruel
picture of Parisian low life."

12   O. Métenier, *La Casserole*, Tresse et Stock, 1889, p. 31.
"A whore I may be, any time . . . But not a thief!"

13   *Le Théâtre Libre*, II (1889), pp. 4–5.
"The dramatic and literary movement brought about by such an
outlet will be appreciated if one recalls that, in the present season
alone, forty acts have been performed, including ten in verse,
while in the same period not a single new act of verse drama was
performed in a Paris theatre. One is therefore justified in stating
that, far from having become the stronghold of naturalism, the
Théâtre Libre is today one of the very few refuges of French
poetry."

14   *Le Théâtre Libre*, II (1889), p. 19, p. 24.
"Who knows but that from this piping-hot production steeped in
contemporary life may not come the plays that everyone is demanding, in the state of lassitude and boredom that has invaded
the present-day theatre?"
"Is there any need to recall the twenty identical efforts that have
blossomed forth in Paris itself, in the last two years, after the
success of the Théâtre Libre, and which may one day be capable of
supplying new outlets for young dramatists?"

15   See especially Jullien's own selection of Press comments in the
preface to his book *Le Théâtre vivant*, Charpentier-Fasquelle, 1892.

16   *Art et Critique*, III (1892), p. 89.
"A masterpiece of carefully detailed psychology and skilfully
handled emotion, with in each scene the interplay of laughter and
tears, the grotesque and the tragic, as in life, for Salandri, whose
ironic and shrewd observation cuts across all conventions, *is not of
the sordid-realist school.*"

17   See, for instance, J. Ernest-Charles, *Le Théâtre des Poètes*, Ollendorff, 1910, p. 164, pp. 172–173.

18   E. Brieux, *L'Engrenage*, Tresse et Stock, 1894, p. 113.
"Because it's like a set of gear wheels, once you stick your finger
in there, you just can't help being dragged right through."

19 Antoine, "*Mes Souvenirs*", p. 219.
"A committee of poets has been formed to set up an Art Theatre which will soon be giving . . . plays by Pierre Quillard, Rachilde, and Stéphane Mallarmé. This is excellent, for the Théâtre Libre is not enough any more; other groups are becoming necessary to perform certain works which we cannot produce here. I don't see it as competition but as a complement, now that the development is accelerating."

20 "*Mes Souvenirs*", pp. 291–292.
"To tell the truth, I really feel, too, from the artistic point of view, that we are getting to the end of our tether and that our movement is nearing its end. For the last two years I have had to fall back on foreign drama, on sensational curiosities, to fill in the gaps between our real performances, but that is all running out. The season has really only brought *Boubouroche*, and the immense stir caused by *The Weavers* was, in fact, no more than a repetition of Tolstoy or Ibsen."

21 *Le Théâtre Libre*, V (1893), p. 21.
"I would like to try and convince you . . . that actors never know anything at all about the plays they are called upon to perform. Their job is quite simply to perform them, to interpret as best they can characters whose conception is beyond them. The intellectual gulf between the writer and his interpreter is so insuperable that the latter never completely satisfies the former."

V

THEORY AND PRACTICE OF REALISM

ANTOINE WAS THE FIRST and most successful avant-garde practitioner of realism, but he was not, of course, the only one. Several of the little theatres of the early avant-garde were at some stage associated with realism or naturalism as a means of reinvigorating the theatre, and the literary reviews of the period abound in theoretical articles and discussions on dramatic realism. These articles often serve as a prelude to projects for founding new theatres, and are an essential part of the ferment which eventually led to the transformation of the French theatre.

Typical of such periodicals was the *Revue d'Art Dramatique*, a fortnightly review which first appeared in 1886 and continued to be published throughout the period of the first avant-garde. It is interesting, therefore, not only because it provided a forum for the young generation of would-be naturalist dramatists, but also because it clearly reveals the trend *away* from naturalism which set in after the first successes of Antoine and others, and shows up the limitations as well as the virtues of stage naturalism. At the same time the *Revue d'Art Dramatique* remains a predominantly traditionalist publication, and tends to support the then orthodox view of the theatre as primarily an 'industrial' activity with, for example, articles which attempt to extract the principles of dramatic writing from an analysis of the plays of Dumas or Augier. When the new note of revolution is sounded it is therefore all the more striking in this orthodox context.

Already in 1886 there are a few notes of originality: an article protests at the seemingly indispensable presence in every play of the *personnage sympathique*; attacks the evils of censorship as it was then practised; and welcomes the vigour and originality of the plays of Henry Becque. But the only important clue, among scores of other articles, to the presence of the generation of young authors who were shortly to transform the theatre is in the conclusion to an article by one Albert Guinon, on realism in dramatic style and the need for a reform of stage dialogue. He gives a brief, embryonic idea of the new partisan attitude which could stand as the *credo* for the whole of the avant-garde:

> Voilà ce qui nous frappe tous, nous les nouveaux venus dans cette période de souffrance et de transition. Nous sommes à l'heure de nos débuts, le seul moment où l'on voit clair et où l'on parle sincèrement. Plus tard, quand on a déjà son passé, le bon théâtre n'est plus celui qu'on voudrait faire, c'est celui qu'on a fait.[1]

The *Revue d'Art Dramatique* thus provides a forum where ideas and theories meet and multiply. A frequent contributor, Fernand Lefranc, puts the case for the new avant-garde in an article entitled "Le Théâtre et les jeunes Auteurs", which appeared in 1887. He contends that it is already widely recognized that some kind of reform of the theatre is most desirable and that too few plays by young dramatists are reaching the stage. However, whereas young authors often complain that it is impossible to have their works performed, Lefranc maintains that the young writers of the day have excellent opportunities, and counts the period one in which "the ways are open, and each is free to choose his own"—precisely because the drama so obviously leaves much room for improvement.[2] Lefranc then expounds at some length the limitations of the currently recognized leaders among the dramatists, and concludes that the theatre is antiquated and sterile. The result is that really original new drama would be enthusiastically received by intelligent and cultivated people, in spite of the fact that such an audience is no longer discernible in the crowd of contemporary theatre-goers. The discriminating audience of the seventeenth and eighteenth centuries has been superseded by a semi-literate public saturated with vaudevilles and feeble witticisms. Lefranc concludes:

> Malheureusement l'audace manque aux jeunes gens. Aux chutes retentissantes et qui ne sont pas sans gloire, ils préfèrent les succès faciles qu'on oubliera demain. Le public les entretient dans cette erreur, et on lui sert la littérature qu'il mérite.
> Les jeunes gens secoueront-ils la torpeur qui les envahit? Oseront-ils, un jour, aborder les grands sujets? Un public digne

d'entendre des chefs-d'œuvre sortira-t-il de la foule? Tout le monde l'ignore.[2]

The imminent burst of activity among the dramatists of the new generation was evidently not yet visible. As for the new audience, in spite of Lefranc's remarks it is doubtful whether the avant-garde were really conscious of any attempt to attract new customers into the theatre (in the way that Vilar, Planchon, and others have done since the War) and doubtful, too, whether their activities, in fact, attracted the attention of anyone not already an actual or potential customer of the commercial theatre. The idea of appealing, for instance, to a working-class audience simply did not occur, hardly even, it seems, to the supporters of the Théâtre d'Art Social, described later in this chapter. Their preoccupations were the more obvious ones of reforming stage presentation and dramatic writing.

In 1888 the *Revue* instigated one of many discussions on realism in stage technique. A series of performances was given in Brussels in that year, of plays by Shakespeare and Schiller, by an independent German troupe organized by the Grand Duke of Saxe-Meiningen. Many critics were impressed by the original methods of this semi-professional company, whose intelligent production, especially in the spectacular handling of crowd scenes, was described and widely recommended. Antoine on this occasion wrote a long letter to the leading drama critic, Francisque Sarcey, and the *Revue* published this together with a commentary. The innovations of the Meininger company do not seem very remarkable today: the walking-on players were expected to act, and not merely be seen on stage; principal actors took their turn at playing small parts; crowd movements were planned and rehearsed in detail. Antoine and other observers found many aspects of the Meininger productions unsatisfactory; but the important differences between their methods and anything then existing in the Paris theatre made the younger enthusiasts all the more aware that certain reforms were not only desirable but feasible.

More discussions on the merits of realism appear in the 1889 issues. Léon Hennique's historical drama, *La Mort du Duc d'Enghien*, played at the Théâtre Libre (p. 54), was one of the few successful applications of scientific naturalism to a historical subject. The complaint is voiced that Hennique's method, based on documents and devoted to historical accuracy, inevitably leads to an "untheatrical" product, in that he refuses the artist's prerogative of entering into the minds of his characters and merely conveys the outward reality. While the reviewer admits the inanity of much pseudo-historical drama, he none the less claims that it is necessary to adopt intuitive judgments in constructing a play, and even to stylize the superficial, documentary truth.

"The impossibility of a modern verse drama" is the title of a contribution to the discussion of Jean Aicard's *Le Père Lebonnard*, also played by Antoine (p. 64). Rodolphe Darzens, rather than demonstrating that verse is unacceptable, claims that verse is not plausible in many dramatic situations. He maintains that the tradition whereby verse is obligatory in certain genres (he is thinking of Augier as much as of Aicard, his latter-day imitator) should give way to a new combination of action and poetry, in which the verse form will be an essential and not a decoration.

Another interesting source of theory and speculation is a more openly partisan review, *Art et Critique*, which appeared weekly in 1889 and 1890, under the management of Jean Jullien, and was revived briefly, before finally disappearing, in early 1892. *Art et Critique* is sympathetic to all aspects of progressive opinion, but consistently supports Antoine and the Théâtre Libre, where Jullien had several of his plays performed. In the 1889 volume the most interesting theoretical article is by Gaston Salandri, whose plays are described above (pp. 60–1), and is entitled "La 'pièce bien faite' et le Théâtre Libre". This article marks the difference between the skilfully constructed dramatic mechanisms, the 'clockwork masterpieces' of Dumas, Augier, and Sardou, on the one hand, and what Salandri claims as the typical Théâtre Libre play. The most successful works presented by Antoine have been, so Salandri maintains, those that follow for their plan of construction the natural scheme of action of real life. He traces this method specifically to Zola, whose precept of "l'action telle quelle"— "action just as it is"—is the basis of the whole system. This substitution of a stylization supposedly based on some 'natural' principle, in place of the familiar and successful structures of established dramatists, leads the writer to believe that "nous sommes à l'aube d'un renouvellement de nos moyens dramatiques".[3]

The viability of naturalism on the stage continues to preoccupy the review's contributors. An article appearing in 1890 and entitled "La Raison suffisante" considers the problem of the frequently banal and uninteresting results of a strict representation of reality—for reality itself is often banal—and concludes that the dramatist must interfere with reality to the extent of making the motives of his characters apparent, even though motives in real life are often invisible. This admission of the need for a stylization of some kind—a sympton of the second phase, logically, of naturalistic drama, after the initial impulse of revolt against artificiality has abated—provides the dramatist with an escape from the fallacy of which Zola himself was the victim, and which was the basic weakness of his theoretical views: that is, the notion that realism and reality are in some way identical.

The debate in *Art et Critique* continues with an appraisal of a lecture given at the Théâtre d'Application by Henry Bauer, one of the most influential critics to support the Théâtre Libre and the avant-garde in general. His lecture on "Le Théâtre nouveau", here reported by the editor, Jean Jullien, claims that the development of the new naturalist style of the young generation of dramatists, together with the reforms in acting and production which have been described earlier, marks an important point in the history of theatrical reform. Bauer, approved by Jullien, repudiates the link with Zola, whose plays were conventionalized and represented little of the authentic naturalism of his novels. The line of influence of the 'new theatre' is traced from Henry Becque and through the stages of development of the Théâtre Libre. The principle of the simplicity of dramatic means replaces that of the strict observation of reality, and the idea described above of a limiting stylization is expressed by Bauer in terms of a selection from reality—the precise point, in fact, at which photography becomes an art form. These modifications of the naturalist aesthetic, expressed, after the revolutionary manner of the avant-garde, in terms of a repudiation rather than a development from an inherited tradition, constitute the theoretical framework of the preoccupations of the young realists.

Much the same ideas are later taken up in Jullien's own articles on realism in drama, which eventually formed, together with the texts of his plays, a book which he called *Le Théâtre vivant, essai théorique et pratique.*[4] The crux of his theory is an attempt to combine a refutation of the naturalist theatre, which has "failed", with the borrowing of certain naturalist techniques. A revised version of the naturalists' "slice of life" slogan becomes, not very convincingly, "une pièce est une tranche de vie mise sur la scène avec art",[4] which begs the question and leaves the whole problem of stylization unresolved. Jullien is not prepared to define his ideas more precisely than this; and simply postulates a "synthesis of life" as the basis of a play, no doubt for fear of appearing over-concerned with mere technique as distinct from content (which was the real criticism directed by the new generation at established dramatists). The result is that the theory goes little farther than demanding a "living" representation on the stage. But this in a sense marks an advance on the more imitative Théâtre Libre realism: "Mieux vaut, à mon avis, des êtres vivants dans un milieu factice que des fantoches gesticulant au milieu d'accessoires vrais."[4] This is a shift of emphasis which might perhaps be detected in Jullien's own plays. It is also one example of the trend away from naturalism which begins to be apparent almost as soon as the avant-garde comes into existence.

Evidence of the trend away from naturalism, of the dawn of the idealist reaction, is abundant in the same periodicals quoted above. For instance, the *Revue d'Art Dramatique*, in the volume covering the second quarter of 1891, has not only an article on "L'Illusion au Théâtre", which maintains that complete realism of staging is both possible and desirable,[5] but also two articles on "Symbolisme dramatique", concerned with the potentialities of the many poets now turning to drama, and a contribution by Pierre Quillard the title of which is self-explanatory: "De l'inutilité absolue de la mise en scène exacte".[6] Quillard, author of the Théâtre d'Art production *La Fille aux Mains coupées* (Chapter VI), claims the right to make the theatre "a pretext for dreaming", and the deliberate lack of precision in the directions for the setting of his play at the Théâtre d'Art corroborates this. Hence his contention that "le décor doit être une pure fiction ornementale qui complète l'illusion par des analogies de couleur et de lignes avec le drame".[6] Still in the same volume, an evaluation of the naturalist theatre as a whole stresses the limitations which it seems to impose. Its author, Fernand Lefranc, observes the general dissatisfaction with the dramatic products of the great naturalists, and maintains that the dramatist needs a wider field than they allow.

> Le souci de ne mettre au théâtre que des hommes d'aujourd'hui et la prétention de placer toujours les spectateurs comme en pleine réalité . . . c'est s'interdire ou à peu près tous les grands sujets et se condamner à n'écrire que des drames bourgeois.[7]

This is the same Lefranc who two years earlier wrote enthusiastically of the latest developments at the Théâtre Libre. But this does not mean that he is inconsistent, merely that he is aware of the changing scene around him. At this stage the realist tendency can no longer claim a monopoly of originality, if, indeed, it ever could.

Realism in practice is, of course, best illustrated by reference to the remarkable achievements of Antoine at the Théâtre Libre. But there were others who enjoyed a less lasting success yet who were no less dedicated avant-gardists. These included, in the first, crucial period from 1887 to 1894, the instigators and organizers of the Théâtre Moderne, the Théâtre Réaliste, and the Théâtre d'Art Social.

The original plan to found a Théâtre Moderne was announced, with a considerable fanfare, in March 1890, but its opening, several times postponed, did not take place until December. Its first programmes were unremarkable as far as the avant-garde was concerned, and it eventually developed into an average commercial theatre. Before this happened, however, the Theatre was used by a variety of occasional groups, and some interesting plays were seen there during 1891 and 1892, including one of Lugné-Poe's Ibsen productions for Les Escholiers; one of the Théâtre d'Art programmes, including a Maeterlinck play; and works by Grandmougin and Dujardin, all of which are mentioned in later chapters. By the time Lugné-Poe was looking for a theatre in which to present Maeterlinck's *Pelléas et Mélisande*, in 1893, Paul Fort wrote a summary judgment of the now commercialized Theatre: "Le Théâtre Moderne est un concert maintenant: il n'y a rien à faire là."[8] Before it reached this situation, however, the Théâtre Moderne had enjoyed a reputation for producing original drama. In the first few months of its existence it formed a group called L'Avenir Dramatique, and this produced, in May 1891, a play by a

Belgian novelist and critic, Camille Lemonnier, entitled *Un Mâle* and adapted from the author's own novel. This is a Romantic drama in a peasant setting, the story of Cachaprès, a monstrous brute of a man who attracts and at the same time terrifies the women of his village. The atmosphere of the play evolves from one of festive gaiety to one of jealousy and hatred. Finally the brutish hero, not unkind but incapable of gentleness, is hounded out of the village. The play obviously intends to give a stark picture of peasant life, but has to rely on a Romantic freak to be interesting. Thus baldly recounted, it sounds as though it owes as much to the inspiration of Victor Hugo as to that of Zola; but in his time Lemonnier was thought of as a naturalist.

The Théâtre Réaliste

The curious case of Théodore de Chirac, whose performance of his own, over-realistic plays resulted in his being sentenced to fifteen months' imprisonment "pour outrage à la morale publique", is one of the more picturesque by-products of the vogue of *réalisme rosse*. In March 1891 Chirac's play *Prostituée* was included in a programme at the Théâtre d'Art, the poets' theatre recently founded by Paul Fort. Fort later claimed to have produced this play as an effective means of ridiculing the worst excesses of the realists, and the *Théâtre d'Art* magazine refers to *Prostituée* as an outrageous parody of the naturalist manner. It seems, however, that Chirac was serious, and a few months later he formed his own troupe, the Théâtre Réaliste, in the autumn of 1891. It was unfortunate that the founding of this Theatre should coincide with public discussion of a plan to suspend stage censorship for a trial period, since Chirac became the victim of the opponents of this measure. He was sentenced the day before the official commission met to consider the question.

The seven short plays which the Théâtre Réaliste performed in two successive programmes (including a repeat performance of the work seen at the Théâtre d'Art) were quite understandably never published: contemporary comment reveals a variety of reactions. In an article in the periodical *Le Théâtre* Chirac's Theatre is listed with the other progressive groups: "Le Théâtre Réaliste, dont le tenancier, M. de Chirac, nous convia à des scènes d'une intimité qu'effarouche généralement la présence du public . . .

excepté, paraît-il, sur les scènes japonaises."[9] According to the *Annales du Théâtre* for 1891, which adopts a very proper moral tone, Chirac included a particularly scandalous "scène de possession à rideau levé".[10] *Art et Critique* describes the handling of the incident by the enemies of censorship reform, protests that Chirac's sentence was disproportionately severe, and considers that he was merely a morbid exhibitionist.[11] *Art Social* gives a short if unenthusiastic appraisal of two of Chirac's plays, *La Gueuse* and *Prostituée*, with no indication that any enlightened member of the public might find them objectionable.[12]

Little enough information is available on the plays themselves, though the mere titles give some idea: for example, *La Crapule* (*Debauchery*), *La Morte violée* (*Rape of the Corpse*), *L'Avortement* (*The Abortion*). André Antoine notes the incident in his diary, and is furious to find that some provincial newspapers had been informed that the condemnation of Chirac applied to the Théâtre Libre:

> C'est vraiment infâme: une main savante a propagé en province, aussi bien qu'à Bruxelles, sous le titre, en grosses lettres, de 'l'Affaire du Théâtre Libre', que la condamnation de cet imbécile de Chirac à quinze mois de prison, qui ne sont pas certes volés, s'appliquait à nous.[13]

La Plume mentions the first of the Théâtre Réaliste programmes in a brief note: "Ce n'est pas ouvrage de critique que de toucher à l'œuvre de M. de Chirac, mais de vidangeur . . . Nous ne reparlerons plus du Théâtre Réaliste."[14] After the trial, however, *La Plume* considered that Chirac had been unfairly treated, and quoted at length the speech of the defence lawyer, Maître Fernand Labori, who defended *La Plume* in a lawsuit against Péladan and later defended Zola in libel suits arising from his involvement in the Dreyfus case. Labori suggests that the Chirac affair is the fault of society, and blames the "hypocritical modesty" of the public. His defence consists of a succinct survey of the literary trends of the period and the public's reaction to them, and gives an interesting insight into the way public opinion is changing:

> La faute de Chirac, c'est de s'être conduit comme un enfant en présence d'une société qu'il n'a pas comprise. Il n'a pas compris qu'hier tout au naturalisme, elle sera demain tout entière à

l'idéalisme. Dans Zola et son école, il n'a vu que la forme, grossière souvent, sans comprendre ni la psychologie qu'elle cache ni le souffle ardent de la poésie qui est au fond. Il a voulu faire vécu, et comme beaucoup qui ne voient pas qu'il n'y a de vraie vie que dans les choses de l'esprit et du cœur, aveuglé par la matière, il a fait brutal, et le scandale est venu, non de l'immoralité de l'œuvre, mais de la violence de la forme. Ce qu'il a choqué, ce n'est pas la pudeur, c'est le bon goût d'un public avide de sensations raffinées.[15]

The Théâtre d'Art Social

This ephemeral theatre group, like several others of the period, was supported by its own club and periodical review. The review *L'Art Social*, while professing eclecticism, was founded on the basis of the "socialist idea", and during its brief existence from late 1891 to early 1894 its supporters saw in it a weapon in the battle for the establishment of the literature of the future, destined to be "useful literature". The first page of the first issue sets the tone:

> Revue de l'art libre et indépendant, sans chefs ni poncifs, l'*Art Social* est ouvert, aussi largement que possible, à toutes les bonnes volontés. Il est ouvert à tous ceux qui, las de toujours fourbir l'épée sans combattre, auront le courage de mettre leur vaillance et leur talent au service de l'idée socialiste.[16]

This aggressive introduction illustrates the attitude of a militant group of would-be socialists, whose affiliations and sources of inspiration obviously lie outside the field of literature. The group itself, under the name of "Club de l'Art Social", was formed two years before the review, in 1889. But the editor, Gabriel de la Salle, and his colleagues started their experiments in applying socialism to literature at a time when, as we have seen, important changes were taking place in the theatre; and in due course the group formed its own little theatre, with all the features of the avant-garde.

The regular reviews in *L'Art Social* show a marked sympathy for the Théâtre Libre, as might be expected, but also give a fair account of the activities of other avant-garde groups. The main interest of the periodical, however, lies in the account of the planning of the Théâtre d'Art Social. The statutes of this Theatre

were published as early as February 1892, with detailed administrative arrangements. Eventually the Theatre gave its first—and
only—performance in March 1893, and beyond this the vast
possibilities of the project were never transformed into practical
terms. The ambition of the group was to produce a theatre bound
by no aesthetic restrictions but devoted solely to the revolutionary cause. An accompanying note to the statutes of 1892
adds:

> Son but, modeste encore puisqu'il ne s'agit pour le présent que
> de la production d'œuvres socialistes, est très élevé. Il ne vise à
> rien moins qu'à acheminer les esprits vers le théâtre humain, le
> grand théâtre populaire, libre de toutes entraves et gratuit qui
> sera l'œuvre du XXᵉ siècle.[17]

The single performance given in March 1893 began with a verse
prologue written for the occasion by Jean Richepin, at this time a
well-known and successful poet and dramatist, whose works were
played in the national theatres and elsewhere, and who was something of a patron to the group. Following this came a short play by
Séverin Lepaslier, *Reconquise*, which has left little trace: from contemporary accounts it appears to have been the story, with socialist
overtones, of a deceived husband who forgives his wife. It really
is quite extraordinary that the theme of marital infidelity should
continue so to fascinate writers of this period. The main item on
the programme was a three-act socialist play described as a
"revolutionary synthesis", *La Cloche de Caïn*, by Auguste Linert,
and the evening ended with the recitation of an ode to liberty by
Gabriel de la Salle, editor of *L'Art Social*.

Auguste Linert had already had a play performed, in 1890, at
the Théâtre Libre. Entitled *Conte de Noël*, it was declared by its
author to be an attempt to combine realism and mysticism and was
billed as a "modern mystery". The performance was very badly
received, which is hardly surprising in view of the subject. On
Christmas Eve an abandoned farm-girl gives birth to an illegitimate child, which, in despair, she proceeds to murder (off stage).
She then returns to announce that the remains have been gobbled
up by the farmer's pigs, while the neighbours go off to midnight
Mass. It is conceivable that the author may have derived some
benefit from writing such a revolting play, but the audience can

have found little more in it than a lesson in psycho-pathology. That it should have been performed at all can only be explained by Antoine's naïve enthusiasm for anything violent and his occasional strange lapses of taste.

Linert's *La Cloche de Caïn*, therefore, seems to mark some advance on *Conte de Noël*. The text has not survived, but it is hard to imagine any play leaving as unpleasant a taste as his Christmas story. The programme describes *La Cloche de Caïn* as a symbolical exposition of the revolt against capitalism, the three acts being entitled "Pour la patrie", "Vox Populi", and "La Cloche". The main item of the stage properties is a large safe, and the central characters are Mangeor, a banker, the glib and eloquent De Ritch, and Rêve-Azur, Mangeor's employee, a poet and dreamer. The programme brochure includes an article by Linert in which he attacks the decadents and contends that art must function in the service of humanity. He then presents his play and explains his approach and method as a dramatist:

> Après le journal, la revue et le livre: la polémique vivante, le théâtre. *La Cloche de Caïn* qui sonnera les matines de cette manifestation nouvelle [of the new socialism] est un symbole coulé exprès dans le moule revendiqué par nos détracteurs . . . Je n'offre pas une étude *logique* de certains caractères, le calque brut d'un coin de la nature, le côté plastique d'un épisode, l'analyse d'un fait, la suite d'une intrigue, la *tranche de vie* ou *la scène à faire*. La succession des tableaux de ma pièce est illogique de parti pris, l'intrigue est fantaisiste, les caractères sont vagues, les incidents faux, le développement est contre nature et les personnages sont des fantoches agités par des ficelles qui, loin d'être dissimulées, sont en évidence et toutes indiquées, car elles sont nécessaires; mieux encore, indispensables à l'action. Je n'avoue pas des faiblesses, je défends une méthode. Car, pour cette pièce, je pars de cette définition: le théâtre est de l'humanité artificielle.[18]

This rather muddle-headed theory is one of the more extraordinary end-products of the attempt to escape from the limitations of naturalism. By conventional standards the Théâtre d'Art Social, with its single performance and its short-lived review, must be considered a failure. But in the context of the avantgarde the spirit and intention are just as important as practical success. In the avant-gardist's philosophy it is better to travel hopefully than to arrive.

Writers in *L'Art Social* continue to be concerned with the future development of drama, and in particular with establishing the seriousness, the utility, of the theatre, freeing it from the inanity of the entertainment habitually served to a bourgeois public. Its positive critical function is to be combined with an appeal to a popular audience, for whom the theatre is seen as a means of instruction. *L'Art Social* is violently opposed to 'art for art's sake'; insists that the theatre must be a reflection of its age, and thereby a critical commentary of the present social situation; and believes in the value of the theatre as a vehicle for educating the masses and for preparing the future revolution. In an article devoted to "les Primitifs au Théâtre" we again find Auguste Linert speculating about the nature of drama, in terms which seem to owe something to the Hegelian notion of the dialectic. He writes that three stages are perceptible in the drama. The primitive theatre, of which ancient Classical tragedy is the model, is based on a "reflex action"; once the plot is set in motion, Linert believes, a series of tirades and explanations lead it to its conclusion. The second manner, the theatre of action, is said to be that of both Romantics and Realists; it seems to Linert very difficult, in this style based entirely on represented action, to avoid reducing the plot to melodrama. The third and ideal dramatic form, the synthesis, presumably, of the historical process, is hardly recognized yet: it is impressionistic and implies an inspired observation of society coupled with a subtle exposition: "procédé psychologique, par excellence, de l'anxiété".[19] That such theorizing is lacking in clarity does not seem to have worried the promoters of *L'Art Social*; indeed, they welcomed anything which promised to further the cause of reform, as witness the advance announcement of the artistic aims of their Theatre:

> Libre, le Théâtre d'art social n'impose aucune esthétique, aucune vision d'art à ses membres . . . Il admet donc, non seulement la critique de la société bourgeoise, non seulement les luttes contre les préjugés, les ridicules, les abus et les vices, mais aussi l'étude des manifestations passionnelles de l'être humain et les conceptions de l'avenir.[20]

It is evident from such statements that the socialists' ideas on art were not usually very closely defined. They do, however, add a new note to the growing chorus of writers, realists and others, determined to reform the theatre.

Notes

1 A. Guinon, "Le Style au Théâtre", *Revue d'Art Dramatique*, II (1886), p. 44.
 "This is what strikes us, all those of us who are the newcomers in this period of suffering and transition. We are at the time of our beginnings, the only time that one sees clearly and speaks sincerely. Later, when one already has one's past, good theatre is no longer the sort one would like to do but the sort one has done."

2 F. Lefranc, "Le Théâtre et les jeunes Auteurs", *Revue d'Art Dramatique*, VII (1887), p. 105, pp. 115–116.
 "Unfortunately, the young lack boldness. Rather than risk resounding failures which are not without a certain glory, they prefer facile successes which by tomorrow will be forgotten. The public sustains them in this error, and is provided with the literature it deserves.
 Will young people shake off the torpor which assails them? Will they one day dare to tackle the great subjects? Will an audience fit to hear masterpieces come forth from the crowd? No-one knows."

3 *Art et Critique*, I (1889), p. 51.
 "we are at the dawning of a renewal of our dramatic means".

4 J. Jullien, *Le Théâtre vivant, essai théorique et pratique*, Charpentier-Fasquelle, 1892, p. 8, p. 90.
 "a play is a slice of life staged with art."
 "For my part I would rather have living creatures in an artificial setting than puppets gesticulating amidst true-to-life stage props."

5 C. van Hasselt, "L'Illusion au Théâtre", *Revue d'Art Dramatique*, XXII (1891), pp. 170 ff.

6 P. Quillard, in *Revue d'Art Dramatique*, XXII (1891), pp. 181 ff.
 "On the utter pointlessness of accurate staging."
 "the décor should be a pure ornamental fiction, completing the illusion by analogies of colour and line with the play".

7 F. Lefranc, in *Revue d'Art Dramatique*, XXII (1891), p. 8.
 "The desire to present on stage only men of today and the pretension of always putting the audience, as it were, in a completely

real situation . . . has the result of depriving oneself, more or less, of all the great subjects and condemning oneself to writing nothing but middle-class plays."

8   Paul Fort, a letter to Lugné-Poe, March 24th, 1893, in Lugné-Poe, *La Parade*, I, Gallimard, 1930, p. 239.

9   F. de Nion, "Les Volontaires du Théâtre", *Le Théâtre*, 16/12/1892, p. 2.
"The Théâtre Réaliste, whose lessee, Monsieur de Chirac, invited us to witness scenes of such intimacy as is generally frightened away by the presence of an audience . . . except, it seems, on the Japanese stage."

10 E. Noël and E. Stoullig, *Les Annales du Théâtre et de la Musique*, Charpentier-Fasquelle, 1891, p. 421.
"possession scene with the curtain up"—*i.e.*, in view of the audience.

11 *Art et Critique*, III (1892), p. 19.

12 *L'Art Social*, I (January 1892), pp. 69–70.

13 A. Antoine, "*Mes Souvenirs*", Fayard, 1921, pp. 254–255 (15/1/1892).
"It really is monstrous: a cunning hand has put it about, in the provinces and also in Brussels, under the headline, in big letters, 'The Théâtre Libre Affair', that the sentencing of that idiot Chirac to fifteen months in prison, which is not a bit more than he deserves, applied to us."

14 *La Plume*, III (1891), p. 386.
"It is no part of a critic's job to have anything to do with the work of Monsieur de Chirac, but rather a job for a scavenger of cesspools . . . We shall not mention the Théâtre Réaliste again."

15 *La Plume*, IV (1892), p. 64.
"Chirac's mistake was in behaving like a child in the presence of a society which he did not understand. He did not understand that while it was yesterday wholly given over to naturalism, tomorrow it will be entirely given over to idealism. In Zola and his school he saw only the form, which is often coarse, without understanding either the psychology which it conceals or the ardent breath of poetry at the heart of it. He wanted to produce something true to life, and like many who do not see that there is true life only in the things of the mind and of the heart, blinded by matter, he produced something brutal, and the scandal arose not from the immorality of the work but from the violence of its form. What he shocked was not the sense of modesty but the good taste of an audience avid for refined sensations."

16 *L'Art Social,* I (November 1891), p. 1.
   "As a review of free and independent art, without set authorities
   or stereotypes, *Art Social* is open as widely as possible to all those
   of good will. It is open to all who, weary of constantly polishing
   the sword without joining battle, have the courage to devote their
   boldness and talent to the service of the socialist idea."

17 *L'Art Social,* I (February 1892), p. 72.
   "Its purpose, modest as yet since for the time being it is a question
   only of producing socialist works, is a very elevated one. It aims at
   nothing less than the bringing of men's minds to the human
   theatre, the great popular theatre, free from all shackles and free
   of charge, which will be the work of the twentieth century."

18 *Théâtre d'Art Social, Spectacle d'essai du 12 mars 1893,* Charpentier,
   n.d., p. 11.
   "After the newspaper, the magazine, and the book: living polemics, the theatre. *La Cloche de Caïn* [*The Bell of Cain*], which will
   ring out the matins of this new demonstration, is a symbol cast
   deliberately in the mould demanded by our detractors . . . I do not
   offer a *logical* study of certain characteristics, a mere carbon copy of
   a corner of nature, the plastic aspect of an episode, the analysis of
   a fact, the sequence of an intrigue, the *slice of life* or the *great confrontation scene.* The succession of tableaux in my play is illogical by
   design, the plot is whimsical, the features are vague, the incidents
   false, the development contrary to nature, and the characters are
   puppets moved by strings which, far from being concealed, are in
   evidence and even pointed out, for they are necessary, nay, indispensable to the action. I am not confessing to weakness, I am
   defending a method. For my starting-point for this play is the
   definition: theatre is artificial humanity."

19 *L'Art Social,* II (January 1893), p. 9.
   "the pre-eminently psychological process of anxiety."

20 *L'Art Social,* I (February 1892), cover p. 4.
   "Being free, the Social Art Theatre does not impose any aesthetic,
   any vision of art on its members . . . It admits therefore not only
   criticism of bourgeois society, not only the struggle against prejudice, ridicule, abuse, and vice, but also the study of the manifestations of passion in the human being and conceptions of the
   future."

VI

PAUL FORT AND THE THÉÂTRE D'ART

AS ANTOINE AND OTHERS had already suggested, by 1890 it was clear that some kind of "poets' theatre" was needed, not so much in competition with the Théâtre Libre and other realist groups but rather as a complement to them. The Théâtre d'Art constituted just such a theatre, intended originally to play the works of the young symbolists, but soon discovering a predilection for any subject that appealed to the poetic imagination. The group led by Paul Fort was the only one, until the foundation of the Théâtre de l'Œuvre, which the critics treated on anything like equal terms with the Théâtre Libre, since for a time it managed to produce a comparable number of programmes.

The original group, entitled the Théâtre Mixte, was formed by Paul Fort when, aged seventeen, he was still a pupil at the Lycée Louis-le-Grand in Paris. After one performance, in June 1890, the Théâtre Mixte was reinforced by the co-operation of another young poet, Louis Germain, and his friends, who had announced the founding a few months earlier of their Théâtre Idéaliste but had not so far produced anything. With these new participants the Théâtre Mixte gave a second performance in October. Thereupon Paul Fort broke with Germain, and re-formed his group under the new title of Théâtre d'Art, which from November 1890 to March 1892 gave a series of seven programmes. The group's activities ceased when financial losses became too great, but a revival was planned a year later, with financial support offered by a wealthy patron of the arts, Madame Tola Dorian. Although the revival did not materialize, it proved to be the initial impetus in persuading Lugné-Poe to produce *Pelléas et Mélisande*, and this production led in turn to the founding of the Théâtre de l'Œuvre.

When Germain announced his plans for the Théâtre Idéaliste he published the details in a manifesto which appeared in *Art et Critique*, although this was predominantly a review with naturalist sympathies. Germain predicts the death of naturalism and fore-sees the advent of a new medieval epoch in which mysticism will again be a valid basis of literary and philosophical activity, and in which the theatre will once again have the importance and vitality that it enjoyed five centuries ago. This 'idealist' theatre, designed to be parallel to the naturalistic Théâtre Libre and complementary to it, is to have a specifically escapist intention, the achievement of happiness through the pleasure afforded by art. "We shall perform Verlaine, *and* Mendès, *and* all those who have some talent and desire a better state of humanity."[1] The new idealism is not only a necessary escape from naturalism, but its logical consequence:

> Car l'évolution naturaliste n'est pas achevée et l'œuvre natura-liste est le plus puissant agent de l'idéalisme. Le naturalisme est la constatation de la douleur humaine, comme l'idéalisme en est la pitié. . . . Et avoir pitié, n'est-ce pas être, en puissance, un poète?[1]

Among the writers in whom Germain and his friends seek inspi-ration are, first, Villiers de l'Isle-Adam; after him, both psycho-logical novelists and symbolist poets:

> Il nous plaît d'imaginer une transfiguration de la vie réelle dans l'art. Bourget n'a-t-il pas commencé l'œuvre? Loti, Rod, Morice, Verlaine, Remacle ne sont-ils pas avec nous?[1]

The name-dropping and mixture of allegiances are accompanied by a repudiation of most of the existing theatre. Finally the idealists' impatience to make their mark is echoed in an appeal to "all young dramatists wishing to see their plays performed".

The first two Théâtre Mixte programmes were singularly amateurish affairs, and those reviews that noticed them did not in general take them seriously. The second one included a short verse play, *Caïn*, by Charles Grandmougin, who later appears (Chapter VIII) as a protagonist of religious drama, and a play by each of the joint leaders, Paul Fort and Louis Germain. Fort's *La Petite Bête* is an unpretentious joke: "les personnages s'appellent Horace et sont pour le moins barons, c'est tout dire".[2] The "petite bête" is Jeanne, Horace's ingenuous wife. Germain's *François Villon* was a more substantial play, and was later revived by the Théâtre d'Art, after Germain's untimely death, in the spring of 1891, at the age of twenty-two.

Many of the later, more substantial programmes of the Théâtre d'Art, to give it its revised title, proved to be just as amateurish in their presentation as these first experiments. Indeed, the major failing of the Theatre was in the inadequacy of its actors, and in its production, with a few exceptions, especially Lugné-Poe's productions of Maeterlinck. In a retrospective article this "quaint little theatre" was summed up as:

> Le Théâtre d'Art, d'une pénurie légendaire, théâtre cocasse où l'on se mettait en quête du décor le matin de la représentation, où les interprètes passaient leur temps à courir après de chimériques costumes et de non moins chimériques cachets.[3]

But in spite of such failings in organization and acting, which contributed to the Theatre's final downfall and which would soon have made its survival impossible had not financial considerations already done so, the Theatre made an impact during its short existence out of all proportion to the real merits of its organizers. Paul Fort is in no sense comparable with Antoine or Lugné-Poe as actor, producer, or leader of a theatre (though he was seconded by Paul Larochelle, who eventually took over Antoine's functions after organizing the Théâtre de la Rive Gauche). The reason for his success is the simple one that in 1890 there was room for much more avant-garde theatre than Antoine or his minor imitators were able to provide, and in such a situation any original venture was likely to be sympathetically received. The fortunes of the Theatre were also to a large extent due to its symbolist affiliations; with the decline of naturalism, the contributions of the symbolist poets were the most important element in this first stage of the idealist reaction.

The first evening of the new Théâtre d'Art, in November 1890, began with two short sketches from the posthumous volume of drama by Victor Hugo, *Théâtre en Liberté*. Of the other three short plays the only one worth a mention is *La Voix du Sang*, by Rachilde. One of the rare women writers of the period, Madame Rachilde's name turns up again in the programmes of the Théâtre de la Rive Gauche and the Théâtre de l'Œuvre. The play is an ironical picture of a complacent, middle-class couple who take no interest in an incident occurring outside in the street, which turns out to be a murder. Too late they discover that the unheeded cries for help came from their own son. This deliberately banal story with a cruel twist at the end might perfectly well have figured in a programme at the Théâtre Libre.

The second *spectacle* of the Théâtre d'Art attracted much attention, for it was devoted to a translation of the reputedly 'unplayable' five-act Romantic tragedy by Shelley, *The Cenci*. This, it was recognized, was too much for such inexperienced players; but the prodigious ambitions which such an attempt implied were deemed to be well worth encouraging. This performance, in January 1891, also marks the appearance of the first number of the *Théâtre d'Art* review, or at least the first issue to have survived.[4] It is mainly concerned with Shelley's play, for which it is designed to serve as an advertisement and programme, but also records the earlier programmes of the Théâtre Mixte and Théâtre d'Art and lists a wide and ambitious range of future projects, which are added to in later numbers of the review.

Much, therefore, was expected of the next programme in March 1891, which again was accompanied by an issue of *Théâtre d'Art* containing texts and comments, and although the evening included poetry-reading and five very different plays, expectations were not disappointed. An unpublished one-act play by Paul Gabillard, *Les Veilleuses*, appears to have been a strangely evocative, macabre tableau of village women keeping vigil by the corpse of the village bellringer. It was classified as "Maeterlinckian"; although Maeterlinck was performed for the first time two months later, his first plays had been published the previous year.

The most striking play of the evening was *La Fille aux Mains coupées*, by Pierre Quillard, the text of which appears in the *Théâtre d'Art* number mentioned above. This is a slight verse dialogue, not at all theatrical, which evokes the symbol of the refusal of sensual love and the chaste aspiration towards spirituality:

> Supposez une légendaire fiction dramatique récitée par une voix terrestre, qui ne traduirait les au-delà d'un rêve et ne les matérialiserait que juste assez pour en filigraner la trame sur un fluide fond d'or, et vous entreverrez comment il faut juger l'action de cette pièce.[5]

Thus wrote an apologist of Quillard's *mystère*, of which the author himself states on the first page: "The action takes place anywhere and rather in the Middle Ages." The average reviewer found in this play a "hermetic symbolism", an "interesting . . . but fragmentary impression".[6] Certainly Paris had seen nothing remotely like it before. The select audience of the Théâtre d'Art were wildly enthusiastic. Coming at a time when naturalist drama was showing signs of fatigue, Quillard's work struck an entirely new note in the theatre, and this slight play is in a sense a turning-point.

The same programme included another play by Rachilde, *Madame la Mort*, a hybrid affair described as a "drame cérébral en trois actes". The author herself writes about the play in *Théâtre d'Art*, believing that the limited resources of the Theatre might render some preliminary explanation necessary:

> Les premières scènes du drame se déroulent *quelque part dans la vie*; mais le deuxième acte se passe tout entier dans le rêve, *dans le cerveau d'un homme agonisant* . . . j'ai tâché de rendre palpables certaines hallucinations, telle: la lutte de la *Vie* et de la *Mort* qui se disputent tantôt le corps, tantôt l'esprit du névrosé.[7]

The first act describes how a spoilt, blasé, melancholic artist, Paul Dartigny, smokes a poisoned cigar—this is the supreme egoism of lucid suicide—and the second takes place in Dartigny's own mind, where, as in a dream, he fights in vain against a veiled figure who turns out to be death; in the third act, back in Dartigny's study, he is dead, and his friend and mistress between them settle his affairs in a matter-of-fact way. This was seen as an interesting attempt to combine realism and the supernatural, but failed to make its full impact, as its author had feared, because of the inadequacy of the presentation.

The last item of this remarkably varied evening, after an insignificant "mystical mime" and some poetry-reading, including Mallarmé's *Le Guignon*, was the violently realistic play *Prostituée*, by Théodore de Chirac, already mentioned (p. 81), which Paul Fort later claimed to have included as a means of ridiculing *réalisme rosse*.

In May 1891 the Théâtre d'Art gave its next performance, organized as a benefit for Paul Verlaine and Paul Gauguin. The issue of *Théâtre d'Art* produced for the occasion is the most interesting of all the numbers of the review to have survived. It at once makes clear the affiliations of the Theatre, from its subtitle: "Under the patronage of Stéphane Mallarmé, Paul Verlaine, Jean Moréas, Charles Morice, Henri de Régnier". One of the reasons for including so many poems in a magazine concerned with the theatre is given thus:

> Le Théâtre d'Art, essentiel théâtre des Poètes, s'est fait leur interprète en organisant ce Bénéfice [for Verlaine and Gauguin]. Tous ne pouvant, par des œuvres théâtrales y participer activement, le *Théâtre d'Art* s'est fait un devoir de publier ici des œuvres de ceux qui auront lutté le plus fructueusement pour la proche Renaissance.[8]

The language and manner are characteristic of the avant-garde: fighting analogies, implicit faith in the efficacy of revolutionary action.

This is the longest issue of *Théâtre d'Art*, and runs to twenty-four pages (most of the others being only four or eight pages long). It contains a score or more symbolist poems and a long list of dramatists who figure in the group's plans for the next season, of which the following are only a selection: Marlowe, Shelley, Corneille, Musset, Villiers de l'Isle-Adam, Aeschylus. Plays are promised from numerous contemporary poets identified or associated with the symbolist movement. It also includes a long series of reflections by Mme Rachilde on the "idealist" sympathies of the group, entitled "De la Fondation d'un théâtre d'art".[9] The term "idealist" is, of course, a singularly vague one; and Rachilde herself here admits: "I do not know what school I belong to, I have no aesthetic system." But the essential common feature of the beliefs of this important new group is their opposition to the excessive realism by now firmly associated with the typical dramatists of the Théâtre Libre. (As with the Théâtre Libre itself, the point of departure seems to be the negative one of opposition to all that has gone before.) Rachilde goes on to describe an imaginary encounter with a critical member of the audience at a previous performance of the Théâtre d'Art, "*l'Inconnu* très distingué, le Monsieur de bon ton, le porte-voix spirituel des foules bêtes."[9] This gentleman in a series of conversations formulates a number of exasperatingly reasonable objections to the efforts of the Théâtre d'Art group: they have no money; the simplicity of their presentation is too demanding; "la salle Duprez était trop petite, continua-t-il d'un ton dogmatique, celle-ci [out at Montparnasse] est trop éloignée du centre. Et puis, pourquoi jouer une pièce en quinze tableaux [Shelley's *Cenci*]? C'est se moquer de nous."[9] This leads to a nightmarish dream in which the author is pursued by the innumerable material and moral difficulties that beset the creators of a new theatre, the quarrels, the defections, the accusations of partisan bias.

In a more reasoned and less lyrical passage Rachilde then recognizes the immense progress achieved by the Théâtre Libre, acknowledging that at one time it was the enlightened interpreter even of idealist poets, but defends the idea of the new Théâtre d'Art as a "temple", which tomorrow will be the theatre of Verlaine, of Maeterlinck, of Mallarmé, Charles Morice, Moréas, Henri de Régnier, Viélé-Griffin; "et nous n'aurons plus la très ennuyeuse corvée d'aller *croquer le fœtus* derrière un rang de chapeaux à plumes trottoiresques".[9] This splendidly scurrilous stuff leads the author to welcome the decline of the supposed "Théâtre Libre manner", and she adds the happy news that a Monsieur de Chirac has produced an outrageous parody of it (poor Chirac seems to have come in for a roasting all round, quite apart from his prison sentence later in the year). "On lancera le mot de Cambronne, la plus haute expression de l'art naturaliste, et nous aurons la paix."[9] The final observation on the Théâtre d'Art, still in its early stages, is simply that "fondateurs, auteurs, acteurs et spectateurs, nous ignorons ce qui sortira".[9]

The actual programme at the Verlaine–Gauguin benefit night was again a long and varied one. Much of it was devoted to the recitation of verse—Lamartine, Hugo, Baudelaire, Banville, Edgar Allan Poe—and of the four plays presented, only one was significant: *L'Intruse*, the first of Maeterlinck's plays to be performed, which proved to be of the greatest importance. This performance, in which Lugné-Poe took part, and the presentation seven months later of Maeterlinck's *Les Aveugles* are the most considerable achievements, dramatically, of the Théâtre d'Art. The strange and powerful impression of Maeterlinck's deceptively simple plays is based on the systematic suggestion, rather than expression, of the occult and the sinister. In *L'Intruse* a woman is dying, and in the next room her relatives are gathered, desperately trying to break the awful silence of waiting with disconnected odds and ends of conversation. In a crescendo of unexpressed terror the family sit until the arrival of an invisible stranger—Death—whom only the blind grandfather perceives. A man appears from the next room and indicates, with the sign of the cross, that the woman is dead. The technique of suggestion in *L'Intruse* naturally left room for a variety of interpretations; and in *Les Aveugles*, where all the characters but one are blind, while it was clear that Maeterlinck intended this blindness to be a symbol, his contemporaries were unable to agree on what it symbolized (on any level, surely, one of the beauties of symbolism!). Almost all agreed, however, that these short plays were a remarkably vivid evocation of the supernatural.

Until the programme of December 1891, which included *Les Aveugles*, the Theatre produced nothing new, although in August it repeated some of its more successful productions—*L'Intruse*, Quillard's *La Fille aux Mains coupées*, and *François Villon*, by the late Louis Germain—at a performance given in Asnières, outside Paris in the western suburbs. This curious episode, out of season and out of town, looks to have been virtually a private performance. Curious because no theatre-goer would expect to find anything of significance outside a well-defined area of central Paris. This was a habit, or prejudice, which the first avant-garde reformers did not succeed in changing, or, indeed, ever think of changing. The notion was universally accepted, without question, that French theatre was virtually synonymous with the theatre in Paris; and one must look to the period since 1945 to find this notion seriously challenged. But the *théâtre de la décentralisation*, which has made such remarkable progress in the last twenty years, is the work of another generation of the avant-garde, with other preoccupations.

Back in Paris in December, the Théâtre d'Art group followed up the success of *L'Intruse* with their second Maeterlinck play, *Les Aveugles*. Although this performance was less successful than the first, *Les Aveugles* was none the less the outstanding play of the five presented at this evening. A group of twelve blind people from an institution are lost in a dense forest. Their mounting fear and apprehension grows through a series of disturbing sounds and signs into general terror, which reduces each one to a state of

panic, in a crescendo movement as in *L'Intruse*. Only at the end of
the play do they discover that the old priest who had been their
guide, and the only seeing person in their world (apart from the
baby of one of the blind women), is lying dead beside them. This
is an allegory of the fate of modern man, for he is blind to meta-
physical reality, his faith lost, and his only function to wait for
death. The originality of this play, written in simple language, lies
in its combining different levels of interpretation, layers of significance, which for many of Maeterlinck's contemporaries were
profoundly disconcerting. The simplicity of the presentation, the
complete absence of action (Maeterlinck himself later described
this as static theatre), the evocative use of sounds, combined to
produce a unique theatrical experience.

The Maeterlinck play was only one item of what was again a
surprisingly varied evening. It included *La Geste du Roi*, a modern
adaptation of a medieval verse chronicle, and *Le Concile féerique*,
by the symbolist poet Jules Laforgue, which turns out to be an
ironical little sketch in which an idyllic, moonlit love scene is
interrupted by the arrival of tourists and other bourgeois. The
most interesting item theatrically was another adaptation, but in
this case from the Bible: the *Song of Songs*, adapted by Paul-
Napoléon Roinard, "en huit devises mystiques et trois para-
phrases". This was an original and ambitious dramatic experiment.
The poetic dialogue was accompanied by a complex "orchestration" of music, colour, and perfume inspired by Wagner's attempt
to synthesize the different arts and by the theory of correspondences taken up by Baudelaire and others. Each *devise* was built
upon certain dominant sounds, colours, and music specified in
the stage directions, which appeared with the full text in the
Théâtre d'Art number issued as a programme for the occasion—
for example:

> Orchestration: du verbe: en i luminé de l'o (blanc)
> de la musique: en *do*
> de la couleur: en pourpre clair.[10]

For each scene, to complete the orchestration of the senses, a
different perfume was sprayed over the audience, at least until the
combined effect of several such perfumes became too overpower-
ing. The performance, moreover, took place in an uproar, since

fighting broke out between the symbolists and their detractors; and no-one was able to savour the subtleties of Roinard's correspondences in anything like the spirit of contemplation one presumes was desirable.

This kind of provocative experiment established the Théâtre d'Art as a fighting unit of the avant-garde, but the result is difficult to classify as drama. Such experiments were undoubtedly desirable if only as part of the continuous attempt to extend the limits of possible theatre. But their only literary significance lay in the demonstration of the symbolists' inability to adapt their works to the requirements of the stage. The one notable exception was Maeterlinck, and eventually, of course, Claudel, whose first works were known at this time, but who did not have a play performed until Lugné-Poe produced *L'Annonce faite à Marie*, in 1912.

In spite of the extravagance of the *Song of Songs* production the Théâtre d'Art was able to present two more programmes, in early 1892, before it finally disappeared. The *Théâtre d'Art* review disappeared too, but even its last few issues show no flagging of ambition. Among the long lists of innumerable future projects supporters are promised adaptations and selections from every literature and age: the *Ramayana* and the *Vedas*, *Genesis* and *Exodus*, the *Iliad*, the *Aeneid*, the *Song of the Nibelungen*, Dante's *Divine Comedy*, and Milton's *Paradise Lost*! Among the numerous names of contemporary authors are Rachilde and Maeterlinck, who had already been successfully produced; Ibsen, just 'discovered' by Antoine; and the then unknown Paul Claudel, with a promise to perform his *Tête d'Or*, which was, in fact, never performed during Claudel's lifetime.

The first programme of 1892, after the riotous *Song of Songs* night, began with a lengthy version of Marlowe's *Doctor Faustus*. The choice of this sprawling play, like that of Shelley, of the *chansons de geste*, and of the Biblical adaptation, is evidence of the Theatre's wide-ranging search for original and imaginative drama. This version of the Faust story was presented in ten tableaux "in prosed verse", whatever that may be. It was followed by a reading of Rimbaud's *Le Bateau ivre*, and the evening concluded with an equally lengthy play by the Belgian Charles van Lerberghe, *Les Flaireurs*. It should be explained that the Théâtre d'Art evenings were renowned for their length, due as much to the lack of organization as to the generous quantities of material produced; this one ended at three in the morning.

Lerberghe's play, written before Maeterlinck's *L'Intruse*, was a similar attempt to evoke the progression of terror at the approach of death, and its influence on Maeterlinck was generally recognized. A girl watching over her dying mother finds a series of visitors calling, each more sinister than the last, the final one being the coffin-maker. In her death agony the old woman has a vision of the Virgin Mary. Like Maeterlinck's play, *Les Flaireurs* may be interpreted realistically—the different interested persons arrive as they sense the approach of death—or symbolically, for the visitors are the messengers of death.

The last, disastrous performance of the Théâtre d'Art took place at the end of March 1892. It was so badly received by the audience, it seems, mainly because of the poor quality of the acting. The two scenes chosen from Schuré's *Vercingétorix* gave only a fragmentary idea of the play, which was a five-act patriotic verse drama with a subsidiary love interest. The key scene (the second of those chosen to be played by the Théâtre d'Art), "the love scene in the Temple of Fire", was no doubt derived from Brünnhilde's love scene in *Siegfried*.[11] The programme also included a stage version of the First Book of the *Iliad*, a subject which again confirms the vast ambitions of Paul Fort and his company, but which the audience were inclined to treat as a parody, in the manner of an Offenbach operetta such as *La Belle Hélène*.

The major work of this last programme was *Les Noces de Sathan*, by Jules Bois. This is a Wagnerian drama of fall and redemption in the form of a verse dialogue. An idealist Satan, the fallen angel, is persuaded to accept the love, both spiritual and physical, of Psyche, the symbol of religious devotion, and in this love he is redeemed. It is described as an "esoteric drama", is written in a variety of verse forms, and consists of a series of dialogues between Satan and Psyche, with a commentary by the chorus, Hermes Coryphaeus, who describes the visions which appear to the protagonists, visions of Adam and Eve, Faust, Mephistopheles, Helen, and others. When Satan finally accepts salvation, or the promise of salvation after further trials, the play ends with an "ineffable voice", which counsels and encourages the lovers: "Soyez unis dans la douleur [et vous serez] les plus glorifiés parce que les plus fous!"[12]

After the worthy realism of the Théâtre Libre the programmes of the Théâtre d'Art transport us into another world, the existence of which could hardly be suspected from an acquaintance with the drama that preceded it. It is a world of the poetic rather than the dramatic imagination, and for a time the poets infused welcome new life into the progressive theatre. The symbolists in general returned to the world of poetry once they saw their dreams melt in the harsh light of the stage, and the inadequacies of the Théâtre d'Art condemned it to an ephemeral existence. Idealist writers, of course, continued to write for the stage, and a number of their works were produced in the theatres described in later chapters. But on the whole the symbolists, following Mallarmé's example, were content to rule in the realm of poetry. His future contributions to the art theatre were more than once announced, by others, but never materialized. Claudel apart—and even then in a different generation, for *Le Soulier de Satin* was written in the 1920's—the promise of the Wagnerian cult was never realized.

Notes

1   L. Germain, "Le Théâtre idéaliste", *Art et Critique*, II (1890), p. 264, p. 263.
"For the naturalist evolution is not complete, and naturalist works are the most powerful agents of idealism. Naturalism is the recording of human suffering, just as idealism is pity for it. . . . And to have pity, is that not to be, potentially, a poet?"
"We like to imagine a transfiguration of real life into art. Did not Bourget start the work? Are not Loti, Rod, Morice, Verlaine, Remacle on our side?"

2   *Art et Critique*, II (1890), p. 647.
"the characters are called Horace, and are barons at least, which just about sums it up."

3   François de Nion, "Les Volontaires du Théâtre", *Le Théâtre* (16/12/1892), p. 2.
"The Théâtre d'Art, of legendary poverty, a delightful theatre

where they set out in search of the stage set on the morning of the performance, where the actors spent their time running round seeking non-existent costumes and equally non-existent wages."

4   The seven surviving issues of this magazine are in the Rondel collection at the Bibliothèque de l'Arsenal in Paris. They are analysed in detail in A. Veinstein, *Du Théâtre Libre au Théâtre Louis Jouvet: Les Théâtres d'Art à travers leur périodique*, Librairie théâtrale, 1955, though Veinstein's classification follows the order of binding in the Rondel volume, not the original order of publication.

5   P.-N. Roinard, quoted by Rachilde, *Théâtre*, Savine, 1891, pp. 286–287.
"Imagine a legendary dramatic fiction recited by an earthly voice, which would translate the things beyond a dream and would materialize them only just enough to trace a filigree weft on a fluid gold background, and you will have a glimpse of how the action of the play must be judged."

6   *Revue d'Art Dramatique*, XXII (April 15th, 1891).

7   Rachilde, in *Théâtre d'Art*, ii (March 1891), p. 1.
"The first scenes of the play take place *somewhere in real life*; but the whole of the second act takes place in a dream, *in the brain of a dying man* . . . I have tried to make palpable certain hallucinations, such as: the struggle between *Life* and *Death*, who fight for possession now of the body, now of the mind of the neurasthenic."

8   *Théâtre d'Art*, iii (May 1891), p. 13.
"The Théâtre d'Art, the essential theatre of the Poets, has made itself their interpreter by organizing this benefit night. Since all could not participate actively by giving theatrical works, the *Théâtre d'Art* magazine has made a point of here publishing works by those who will have fought the most fruitfully for the coming Renascence."

9   *Théâtre d'Art*, iii (May 1891), pp. 11–13.
"the very refined *Stranger*, the Gentleman of breeding, the witty spokesman of stupid crowds." "The Duprez hall was too small (he continued, dogmatically); this one is too far from the middle of town. And then, why put on a play in fifteen scenes? You must be joking."
"and we will no longer have the very boring task of going *foetus-gobbling* behind a row of street-walking feathered hats."
"Someone will lead off with a four-letter word,* the highest expression of naturalist art, and they will leave us in peace."

---

* 'Cambronne's word', *merde* in fact, also alluded to in French as "les 5 letteres", was directed at the enemy, so legend has it, at Waterloo.

"founders, authors, actors, audience, none of us know what will come out of it".

10 "Le Cantique des Cantiques", in *Théâtre d'Art*, v (10/12/1891), which gives the full stage instructions. See also D. Knowles, *La Réaction idéaliste au Théâtre depuis 1890*, Droz, 1934, pp. 157–160. "Orchestration: of the word: in i luminated with o (white)
　　　　　　 of the music: in C
　　　　　　 of colour: in pale purple."

11 See especially D. Knowles, *La Réaction idéalist au Théâtre depuis 1890*, p. 394.

12 J. Bois, *Les Noces de Sathan*, Chamuel, 1892, p. 36. "Be united in pain, and [you will be] the most glorified because the most mad!"

VII

THE YOUNG IDEALISTS:
SOME THEATRES AND THEORIES

JUST AS ANTOINE dwarfed the other practitioners of dramatic realism, so the Théâtre d'Art of Paul Fort dominates the scene at the start of the idealist reaction. The parallel is, however, not altogether correct, for the Théâtre d'Art never attained the pitch of professionalism of the Théâtre Libre under Antoine, was never a serious rival of the commercial theatre, and, indeed, paid for its amateurishness by its early disappearance. It was not until 1893 that a viable poets' theatre came into existence, when Lugné-Poe founded the Théâtre de l'Œuvre, the early months of which are described in Chapter X. Meanwhile others were trying similar ventures, though with less success.

In May 1893, when Charles Léger founded his Théâtre des Poètes, the Press recognized the need for such a theatre.[1] The group thus formed hardly fulfilled its founder's hopes, but this was largely due to a lack of suitable material. There is some parallel here with the Théâtre Libre, which had earlier failed to maintain its promise of eclecticism for much the same reasons. The explanation, or excuse, commonly given is simply that of the scarcity of good poetic drama, as witness the view of the critic Ernest-Charles, in a retrospective book written in 1910:

Le Théâtre Libre recueillait des poètes les œuvres dramatiques les plus diverses, et il ne dépendait de lui que ces œuvres ne fussent susceptibles de renouveler le théâtre poétique.[2]

He then suggests the reason for this when he comes to consider Léger's Theatre:

Le Théâtre des Poètes n'a pu déterminer un courant poétique ou dramatique nouveau. Chaque poète est venu au théâtre avec son indépendance et sa force ... Et l'époque n'est riche et n'est belle que d'individualités brillantes et puissantes.[2]

Whether this view is sound literary criticism is open to argument —it appears to assume that a 'school' or tendency must evolve a recognizable style shared by all its members in order to be dubbed a success, whereas most of us are happy to applaud the brilliant individual, whether he belongs to a school or not, and sometimes precisely because he does not—but it is symptomatic of critical reaction to these theatres. Many commentators found it necessary to put up some such explanation of what they felt to be the (relative) failure of the poetic theatre.

In these terms the Théâtre des Poètes was typical: shortlived, but performing a vital function in avant-gardist eyes. Apart from a number of unmemorable playlets, "lyrical scenes", pastorals, and mimes, the Theatre produced two plays of substance, in November 1893 and January 1894. The first, an "epic drama", L'Empereur, by Charles Grandmougin, is a lengthy series of tableaux in four acts on the life of Napoléon. Reading the play, one has the impression that the prodigious adventures of Bonaparte are handled with conviction and vigour; it seems that the audience at the Théâtre des Poètes found Grandmougin's play singularly dull.[3]

Kèmener, performed in the following programme at the Théâtre des Poètes, is a Breton drama by Eugène le Mouël, known from the late 1880's and for many years as a writer of Breton poetry and stories, though this is his only play. The hero of the title is a hunchback peasant, a persecuted being secretly in love with the fair Katel. In battle, inspired by religious fervour, Kèmener overcomes his physical deformity by his moral strength, and heroically saves Katel and her young lover. He is acclaimed, and dies in anguish as the young lovers prepare to be married. Although this melodrama, reminiscent of the more lurid aspects of Hugo, presents peasants speaking in alexandrines, it is less ridiculous than this may suggest.

A more successful theatre was the one founded in the last year of this initial period of the avant-garde, the Théâtre de la Rive Gauche, which gave its first performance in February 1894 and another in June. It was formed at the instigation of Madame Tola Dorian, and under the artistic direction of Paul Larochelle, who had been a member of Paul Fort's group and later succeeded Antoine. Its first and most remarkable achievement was the first performance of Villiers de l'Isle-Adam's Axël, the breadth and imagination of which had already tempted various progressive groups, though none had gone so far as to play it. Villiers's play had been known for years (parts appeared as early as 1872), but, in accordance with the author's own view, it was widely believed that *Axël* was unplayable. In Larochelle's production it was found that in particular the lengthy philosophical disquisitions of Maître Janus were untheatrical and difficult to follow on the stage. Nevertheless they were listened to with respect and attention by this audience. The Théâtre de la Rive Gauche, performing in Montparnasse, had an audience unlike that of central theatres— even the avant-garde ones—composed predominantly of artists, students, and, it is claimed, workers.[4] This is one of the very few occasions during the whole of this initial period when the idea, so familiar today, occurs of attracting a theatre audience including not only the bourgeois intellectual but others too, from less favoured social backgrounds. Even then, it is no more than a passing reference. The reaction to *Axël*, at any rate, was unusually enthusiastic.

This success was interpreted not only as a sign of the vitality of the progressive theatre groups, but also as one more confirmation of the shift of emphasis towards idealism. The belief that the world is illusion, Janus's apologia of physical renunciation and devotion to cultivating the soul, the suicide of Sara and Axël on the threshold of sublime earthly happiness, all the aspirations to spirituality of Villiers's remarkable play were accorded an intelligent attention that might well not have been found a decade earlier, say, in a similarly enlightened audience. The simple lesson of this event is stated thus in the simple terms of *La Plume*'s reviewer:

> La moralité à tirer du succès d'*Axël* est que le public veut autre chose que les pauvretés d'art qu'on lui sert en ses habituels théâtres. Nous pouvons conclure, en dépit des tâteurs de pouls ordinaires de la foule, que le peuple des spectacles n'est pas si malade qu'on veut bien le dire. De hautes idées, de beaux symboles et du style élevé lui plaisent mieux que de basses intrigues racontées en auvergnat.[4]

In less partisan terms this triumphantly successful performance of a difficult play marks the period from which can be dated the permanent establishment of the avant-garde theatres as a feature of cultural life in Paris. Another contemporary reviewer, in the *Mercure de France*, wrote in terms which might, indeed, stand as the epigraph to any avant-garde venture:

> La représentation d'*Axël* a encore élargi le cercle du possible au théâtre; après un semblable essai tombent d'elles-mêmes les vieilles objections tirées d'antiques usages et de principes académiques.[5]

After *Axël* the experiment of the Théâtre de la Rive Gauche was cut short by Larochelle's new association with the Théâtre Libre. He took over Antoine's functions for a time, and in early 1895 produced among other things Villiers de l'Isle-Adam's *Elën*. Before the end of the 1894 season, however, the Théâtre de la Rive Gauche managed to produce a second programme, including one play of interest, a brief sketch by Rachilde, *Le Vendeur de Soleil*. This is practically a monologue, a neat little scene in which an eloquent beggar on the Pont des Arts, having nothing left to sell to the passers-by hurrying away, "sells" them the view of the sun setting over the Seine, with his picturesque commentary. This is a realistic and ironical picture of the cheap-jack at his trade; but it also contains a more subtle irony, as a symbolical representation of the function of the artist, who reveals the beauties of the world to the average man, otherwise blind to such things.

The idealists—a blanket term covering symbolists, decadents, anti-realists, and others—did not in general evolve any coherent theories of idealist drama. But some of their reflections are worth examining, as they appear in periodicals of the period, for the light they cast on the mechanisms of the avant-garde. The first *Revue Jeune*, started in 1892, but from the following year known by its new title of *L'Art et la Vie*, provides some interesting examples, as does another, later periodical, confusingly enough also called *La Revue Jeune*, which appeared briefly in 1894.

In the first issue (May 1892) of the first *Revue Jeune* the literary editor, Maurice Pujo, explains the ideas behind its foundation, typical of many such periodicals and therefore illustrative of much of the literary activity of the time. He expresses interest in symbolism, but has doubts as to what the term implies in literature. At the same time he and his colleagues on the review believe that any renewal of art must come from a "subjective contact" with life. The abstract basis of this view, expressed in the slogan *l'art et la vie*, which later became the title of the review, is developed at great length. The precepts of artistic creation which it implies are imprecise, but clearly orientated in the direction of a highly personal idealism:

> Il faut d'abord que la vision des choses soit changée; qu'on cesse de les regarder de trop près, de les analyser dans leurs détails et leur matière, pour n'en conserver que des intuitions synthétiques et fortes. Il faudra modifier avant tout la vision de la Femme qui est l'éternel Objet. Les générations précédentes l'ont regardée à la loupe, ils n'ont senti d'elle que ses nerfs répondant à leurs nerfs; ils ne lui ont demandé que des impressions aiguës comme des pointes de feu, mais non la grande chaleur que seule peut donner l'âme.[6]

In a later elaboration of this approach we are offered an explanation of the principle involved: that of giving a new vitality to literature through a renewed, intuitive experience of life. At the same time the part played by foreign influences is acknowledged:

> La vie: ce fut le point de vue moral qui s'éclaira le premier. On connut Tolstoï et les maîtres du roman russe. Les littératures du Nord avec Ibsen, Nietzsche et tant d'autres, nous apportaient un souffle d'action, de vie forte, profonde et violente même, éveillaient en nous le regret de la puissance, que des stimulations factices n'avaient pu nous donner.[7]

In less abstract terms it was, of course, precisely this foreign inspiration which was an important source for the avant-garde dramatists, in revolt against the artificiality of their elders.

In general the theories propounded by the idealists were no more clear or coherent than those described above. The familiar theme continues, in the pages of *Revue Jeune*, for instance, according to which foreign dramatists are seen as the supposed bearers of the truth that so conspicuously escapes native writers. The outstanding foreign influence is still thought to be that of Ibsen. An interesting example is a notice by Pujo of a book just published, *De Scribe à Ibsen*, by René Doumic, a young but influential critic who in later life was an Academician and editor of the

Revue des Deux Mondes. This notice firmly refutes Doumic's supposed contention that Ibsen derives from a line of influence in the French theatre traced, in the words of the reviewer, from Scribe, but omitting the Romantics, and continuing "via Dumas senior, Louis Bouilhet, Augier, Dumas junior, Sardou, Barrière, Lemaître, de Curel, and a few other manufacturers, *boulevard* writers, academicians, and the like".[8] In fact, this is a considerable over-simplification of Doumic's argument, but Pujo further protests against the critic's interpretation of drama in terms of analysis, and also takes exception to his version of the psychological "theatre of ideas". Here at last we begin to get something like the germ of a theory of idealist theatre. Pujo insists that the theatre is a dynamic, creative process, as opposed to one based on study and technique, as the naturalists had contended:

> Peu nous importe la matière traitée; il y a ici une question de méthode; il s'agit de savoir si cette matière, on l'analysera, ou si on l'animera. Ne les laissons pas au moins s'emparer d'Ibsen![8]

On the much discussed question of who should or should not lay claim to Ibsen the *Revue d'Art Dramatique* published an interview with the great man himself, in April 1894, when *A Doll's House* was produced at the Vaudeville, a regular commercial theatre. Ibsen admits possible symbolist interpretations, but protests that commentators and actors see too much symbolism in his plays and maintains that his first aim is to depict live characters.[9] This pronouncement, of course, left the dispute between realists and idealists for the possession of Ibsen as much unresolved as ever; though it possibly contributed to mitigating the exclusiveness of both sides.

In the second periodical to appear with the title *La Revue Jeune*, an ephemeral magazine which lasted only from January to July 1894, we find another characteristic example of the way in which young writers were becoming increasingly preoccupied with the idealist reaction and its incidence on the progressive theatres. By examining their preoccupations and assumptions in some detail one can get a good picture of avant-gardism—defined in terms of the overall situation in 1894—in action.

Some of the articles by the young contributors to *La Revue Jeune* are laboriously concerned with making the more obvious

discoveries about the constraints and requirements of the dramatic medium. But some help to propagate new ideas, and the general
pattern of review and comment conveys the atmosphere of the
many small groups flourishing in 1894, towards the end of the
initial period of the growth of the avant-garde. The compilers of
the review are aware, even in the first number, that it is likely to
be an ephemeral venture; this fundamental instability seems to be
an accepted part of their idea of progress.

The most important of the foreign influences—if one were to
judge from the pages of *La Revue Jeune* alone—is exercised by
Björnson, to whom three distinct articles are devoted, rather than
Ibsen. Adolphe Thalasso (the historian of the Théâtre Libre) gives
a detailed analysis of the Turkish theatre, dwelling on its popular
traditions and the way in which parts of these traditions derive
from ancient legend, parts from Molière. This is not the first
account of the Turkish plays of *Karagueuz* to appear in France (six
years earlier the *Revue d'Art Dramatique* gave an account of a book
on the subject; and shortly before Thalasso's article there was an
illustrated lecture at the Théâtre d'Application), but the writer
here provides a number of details which suggest a parallel between the Turkish traditions, which are appreciated by everyone,
at all levels of society, and certain popular forms of Western
theatre, particularly *Commedia dell'arte* and *Guignol*. This leads to
the belief that in certain popular traditions writers may find the
source of a new vitality of dramatic forms. Thalasso's purpose is
precisely this:

> faire connaître au public français l'esthétique du théâtre turc,
> absolument inconnu en France, et qui par sa verve et son
> humour se rapproche plus que n'importe quel autre théâtre de
> l'Europe du génie de notre scène et de notre vieille gauloise-
> rie.[10]

The same contributor offers a curious project involving both
drama and poetry: the revival of the *cours d'amour* in which poets
declaimed their own compositions. At length he describes his
plans for resurrecting the medieval custom of competitive declamation, with a jury presided by a woman, prizes awarded by
public approbation, and poets submitting their works according
to the established forms of chivalrous tradition. The enthusiasm

which greeted Thalasso's Utopian scheme was considerable. The absence of any widely recognized poets' theatre, "the utter impossibility of poets having their works performed in public",[11] explains the welcome which his article received. The idea of widening the poets' public, of combining it with that of the *chansonnier*, appealed to many writers in search of new and original means of expression.

The picture that comes out of the pages of *La Revue Jeune* is of an avant-garde clearly established in what we now think of as its regular pattern, that of numerous small groups, often existing for a short time only, dispersing their efforts in many directions. René Doumic, the critic who was so severely taken to task by the earlier *Revue Jeune* for his views on Ibsen, acts as literary sponsor to this new magazine and its young organizers, and his introductory remarks in the first issue throw some light on the contradictions which are inherent in the avant-gardist attitude of revolt. The last few years have not been, in his view, simply one of the privileged periods—like that of the beginnings of Romanticism—in which everyone was young in spirit, whatever his age. In spite of the vast numbers of young writers, "l'époque est devenue sceptique et morose, ironique et désabusée".

> Ee cela sans doute est le contraire de la jeunesse. Beaucoup de ceux qui n'ont pas encore vingt ans subissent profondément l'influence de cette atmosphère où ils vivent. On les voit égoïstes et railleurs. Les facultés d'enthousiasme sont celles qui leur manquent le plus; mais en revanche ils sont abondamment pourvus de la faculté dénigrante. Ils n'ont que mépris pour les anciens et pour les vieux. Et les anciens ce sont pour eux tous ceux qui les ont précédés. Et les vieux, dont la vieillesse chenue leur fait pitié, sont parfois tout juste majeurs. Au surplus, ils se haïssent entre eux; ils étonnent par leur férocité.[12]

Doumic is writing here with all the weight and authority of an ancient thirty-four-year-old! The contradictory attitudes of enthusiasm and cynicism—for the writers in this review, for example, are ingenuously enthusiastic—develop alongside the contradictions of different literary schools, and produce a situation in the independent, avant-garde theatres precisely the opposite of that which might favour the growth of a single, well-defined style to replace vaudeville and melodrama.

This period of transition finds contemporary observers with little idea of what the future may produce. Doumic points out:

Le roman naturaliste est un genre épuisé, et le roman de psychologie est déjà une mode d'hier. La comédie de mœurs telle qu'Augier et M. Dumas l'avaient comprise semble aujourd'hui 'vieux jeu'. D'autre part voilà que le genre du Théâtre Libre est déjà un poncif. La poésie parnassienne est morte, et la poésie symboliste n'a pas encore réussi à vivre.[12]

This complicated pattern of relative and changing values, of hesitant experiment and bitter polemics, of alternating doubt and certainty, is the setting in which a ferment of ideas was working to produce the theatre as we know it. *La Revue Jeune*, in the few months of its existence, made a relatively small but typical contribution to the exchange of views necessary to the growth of the avant-garde movement.

Notes

1   See, for example, *Revue d'Art Dramatique*, XXXII (1893), pp. 180–183.

2   J. Ernest-Charles, *Le Théâtre des Poètes 1850–1910*, Ollendorff, 1910, p. 451, p. 458.
"The Théâtre Libre gathered a great diversity of dramatic works from the poets, and it was not its fault that these works were not capable of renewing the poetic theatre."
"The Théâtre des Poètes was not able to determine a new current in poetry or drama. Each poet came to the theatre with his own independence and strength . . . And the riches, the beauty, of the age lie only in brilliant and powerful individualities."

3   See, for example, *L'Art et la Vie*, III (December 1893), p. 845; *La Plume*, V (December 1893), pp. 542–543. For Grandmougin's *Le Christ* see Chapter VIII (pp. 116–117).

4   *La Plume*, VI (1894), p. 153.
"The moral to be learned from the success of *Axël* is that the public wants something other than the artistically poor stuff which it is served in its customary theatres. We may conclude, in spite of those who ordinarily feel the pulse of the crowd, that the theatre-going populace is not so sick as is claimed. High ideas, fine symbols, and elevated style go down better than low intrigues recounted in a broad Auvergne accent."

5   *Mercure de France*, April 1894, p. 358.

"The performance of *Axël* further widened the circle of the possible in the theatre; after a venture like this the old objections based on ancient usages and academic principles simply fall to the ground."

6   *Revue Jeune*, I (1892), p. 12.

"First of all the vision of things must be changed; we must stop looking at them too closely, analysing them in their details and substance, and retain only strong, synthetic intuitions. Above all we must change the view of Woman, who is the eternal Object. Previous generations looked at her under a magnifying-glass; all they felt of her was her nerves responding to their nerves; they asked of her only sharp impressions, like points of fire (ignipuncture), but not the great warmth which the soul alone can give."

7   *Revue Jeune (L'Art et la Vie)*, II (1893), p. 2.

"Life: it was the moral point of view that first became clear. One came to know Tolstoy and the masters of the Russian novel. The literatures of the North, with Ibsen, Nietzsche, and so many others, brought us a breath of action, of powerful, profound, even violent life, awoke in us a nostalgia for power which artificial stimuli had been unable to give us."

8   *Revue Jeune (L'Art et la Vie)*, III (1894), p. 151, p. 153.

"The subject to be treated is of little importance; here there is a question of method; it is a question of knowing whether this subject is to be analysed or whether it is to be animated. At least let's not let them get their hands on Ibsen!"

9   *Revue d'Art Dramatique*, XXXIII (1894), p. 14.

10 *La Revue Jeune (L'Avenir Dramatique)*, No. 5 (1894), p. 206.

"to bring to the attention of the French public the aesthetics of the Turkish theatre, which is absolutely unknown in France, and which by its verve and humour is nearer than any other theatre in Europe to the genius of our stage and our old spirit of Gallic humour."

11 *La Revue Jeune (L'Avenir Dramatique)*, No. 4 (1894), p. 166.

12 *La Revue Jeune (L'Avenir Dramatique)*, No. 1 (1894), p. 5, p. 6.

"The age we live in has become sceptical and morose, ironic, and disillusioned. And that no doubt is the opposite of youth. Many who are not yet twenty are profoundly influenced by this atmosphere in which they live. One sees them egoistic and mocking. The faculties of enthusiasm are those in which they are the most lacking; but on the other hand they are abundantly supplied with the faculty of denigration. They have nothing but scorn for the old ones, the aged. And the old ones, in their view, means all those who have gone before them. And the aged, whose hoary old age they find pitiful, have sometimes only just come of age. What is more, they hate one another; their ferocity is astonishing."

"The naturalist novel is a style which is played out, and the psychological novel is already yesterday's fashion. The comedy of manners as understood by Augier and Monsieur Dumas [*i.e.*, Dumas junior] today seems antiquated. And now, moreover, the Théâtre Libre manner is already a cliché. Parnassian poetry is dead, and symbolist poetry has not yet succeeded in coming to life."

VIII

MYSTICISM, MIME, MARIONETTES . . .

IT IS, of course, possible to see the theatre of the late 1880's and early 1890's in terms of its literary antecedents and allegiances, as marking the end of the naturalist vogue and the beginning of the idealist reaction. These are the sort of terms in which it is usually presented, though even from a purely literary standpoint they inevitably involve some over-simplification. To complete the picture, and at the same time convey something of the atmosphere, the flavour of early avant-gardism, one must also look at other aspects of theatrical activity, some of which will be seen in this chapter. They include some illustrations of the renewed interest in religious and mystical subjects; new stylizations made possible by recourse to mime, puppets, and shadow theatre; and some theories on the theatre of the future.

In early 1890 the revue *Art et Critique* published a notice of a Nativity play, *La Marche à l'Étoile*, produced at the Chat Noir shadow theatre. The surprising success of this production leads the reviewer to deduce that "a wind of mysticism is blowing over Paris".[1] In his preface to the *Annales du Théâtre* for 1892 Jules Lemaître describes the signs which lead him to conclude that a revival of religious drama is taking place in the Paris theatre, not only in the numerous plays concerned with priests and their problems, but in the various modern versions of Mystery plays popular at this time. Lemaître concludes that most of these dramatic essays are examples of "piety without faith"; that only in an age which had lost its sense of true reverence could so much cheap religion find its way on to the stage. He exempts from this judgment, however, a number of plays on Christian themes performed in marginal theatres; and it is in these plays, rather than in the realist study of a modern religious dilemma, that the new influence may be discerned. He is thinking particularly of the puppet plays of Maurice Bouchor, performed at the Petit Théâtre de la Galerie

Vivienne, some of the more serious products of the Chat Noir, and the esoteric drama of Jules Bois, whose *Noces de Sathan* (p. 100) formed part of the last programme at the Théâtre d'Art.

The influence of two minor theatres is predominant in the growth of the religious vogue, the puppet theatre of the Galerie Vivienne and the shadow theatre of the Chat Noir, both of which will be described in some detail later. The key to the popularity of these little theatres seems to have been in the unpretentiousness of their artistic activities. The disarming sincerity and fervour of the plays of Fragerolles and others at the Chat Noir and of Bouchor at the Petit Théâtre are reflected in numerous enthusiastic remarks by various critics, who saw in these modern Mystery plays a fresh and original approach to the theatre, owing nothing to contemporary dramatic forms and offering an escape from over-familiar themes.

The period also saw more ambitious attempts to further the notion of religious or mystical drama, and this area is dominated by four dramatists with a remarkably resounding set of names: Grandmougin, Haraucourt, Dujardin, and Péladan.

Both Charles Grandmougin and Edmond Haraucourt produced a large-scale "Passion play", and these were inevitably compared. They each had these verse dramas performed semi-professionally, but the exceptional nature of their limited performances, in each case planned to take place in the period leading up to Holy Week, and the conditions in which the plays were presented contribute to the propagation of their authors' ideas among the young generation of writers then anxious to incorporate every possible original element into their reforms. The contribution of such individual ventures as *Le Christ* and *La Passion* to the development of the new theatre was certainly taken seriously, as witness the favourable reaction of numerous progressive reviews. But they derived from no well-defined literary source of inspiration, and their final incidence on the avant-garde was perhaps less important than that of many plays which were in some respects inferior but which were presented in a more original or controversial style.

Grandmougin's *Le Christ* was performed at the Théâtre Moderne, in between productions of vaudevilles and other more commercial forms of entertainment, in March 1892, and was successful enough to warrant several repeat performances the following month, with an extra tableau added to depict the Resurrection. Grandmougin was not unknown at this time, having contributed to an early programme at the Théâtre Mixte, in 1890, with his verse play *Caïn*, while back in 1887 the amateur group Les Estourneaulx had performed his *drame antique* entitled *Orphée*. Most critics found *Le Christ* much inferior to Haraucourt's rival Passion play, although the Théâtre Moderne production was said to be much better. Grandmougin's Christ appears as a kind of magician who paralyses the hostile crowd. The whole play is presented in adequate but singularly unremarkable language, well summed up in the judgment of the *Annales* for 1892: "la passion décrite en vers élégants".[2] *Le Christ* was none the less one of the successes of the season, and marks a stage in the new interest in religious drama. Grandmougin continued to indulge his taste for epic themes with his story of Napoléon, *L'Empereur*, seen the following year at the Théâtre des Poètes.

La Passion, by Edmond Haraucourt, was a play of more substance. On Good Friday 1890 the text of this work was recited at the Cirque d'Hiver, by Sarah Bernhardt and two other players. On this first occasion the play had a stormy reception, and towards the end Haraucourt himself was obliged to harangue the audience before they would allow the recitation to continue. A full performance, as opposed to a recitation, was, however, mounted in Holy Week 1891, and again at Easter 1892 (on the second occasion thus competing with Grandmougin's *Le Christ*), in both cases at the Théâtre d'Application. These proper productions were more favourably received, and Haraucourt's handling of the story of Christ's Passion was approved and accepted by enthusiastic audiences.

Commentators saw in Haraucourt's Jesus the influence of Ernest Renan, and much of His character is more like that of a humanist reformer than of the intransigent God. Ernest-Charles attacks Haraucourt for having debased a noble theme, and maintains that his Jesus has "une onction toute renanienne, et une sentimentalité plus moderne encore. Il [Jésus] a la rhétorique caressante d'un prêtre élégant des paroisses mondaines qui a médité les poètes de salon."[3] This summary dismissal of a considerable play needs some qualification. The sense of the dramatic, the vividness of crowd scenes, are still striking to a modern reader,

as are the evocative, if highly coloured, descriptions and trans-
positions of Biblical situations:

Jésus, menant Pierre par la porte ouverte:
                                          Viens voir,
Pierre, les monts rosés frémir dans l'or du soir:
Une ombre violette endort les vallons calmes . . .
Pierre: Je vois.   *Jesus*:
                          Avant que l'aube ait réveillé les palmes
Et qu'un autre soleil monte sur l'horizon,
Tu m'auras renié trois fois.[4]

In the 1920's *La Passion* was revived annually. Haraucourt also
produced a version of *The Merchant of Venice*, entitled *Shylock*,
produced at the Odéon in 1889, and his dramatic poem *Héro et
Léandre* was performed in 1893 at the Théâtre du Chat Noir.

In a different tradition, but part none the less of the wave of
mysticism, are the works of Édouard Dujardin, possibly the most
successful and certainly the most ardent of the Wagnerians, and
described as the man who had seen *Parsifal* more times than anyone else. His trilogy, *La Légende d' Antonia*, was performed between
1891 and 1893. In April 1891, shortly after Haraucourt's Passion
play, the first part of the trilogy, *Antonia*, a *tragédie moderne*, was
performed at the Théâtre d'Application. In June of the following
year the Théâtre Moderne was the venue for the performance of
Part II of the legend, *Le Chevalier du Passé*. The third and final part,
La Fin d'Antonia, was produced in a commercial theatre, the
Vaudeville, in June 1893, at a special (single) performance. *La
Légende d'Antonia* is an attempt by Dujardin to express that universal drama of humanity of which Wagner was the apologist. The
adventures of the courtesan Antonia, progressing through the
destruction of her ideal love, the fall into degradation as a prostitute, the aspiration to purity, and the final acceptance of love as a
function of nature leading to maternity—these are all intended as a
criticism of the renunciation of life and of aspiration to the spiritual. The lesson of the trilogy is in the final acceptance of the laws
of the natural world. This is conveyed in a complex poetic form,
using verbal *Leitmotive* and with characters that are hardly characterized—the lover, the shepherd, the knight. The considerable
impact of Dujardin's three plays, in spite of the unfavourable
reception of some of the more inept parts, is conveyed in a con-

temporary judgment which describes how important a place they occupy in the symbolist movement:

> Toutes proportions gardées, et avec une légère teinte rosée de ridicule, comme tout le mouvement lui-même (c'est déjà un grand honneur d'avoir provoqué quelque chose), elles resteront comme le *Cid* de cette pseudo-école.[5]

The last and most original of the four authors whose names are associated with the new mysticism, like Dujardin a dedicated Wagnerian, was Joséphin Péladan. The Rose Cross or Rosicrucian movement was one of the more important of the many mystical and occultist groups existing towards the end of the nineteenth century, and Péladan was, after Villiers de l'Isle-Adam, the most prominent literary figure to be connected with it. Péladan also assumed the name Sâr, an ancient Babylonian title. He did much to revive interest in the Rosicrucian cult, which in his writings he associated with the cult of the Grail.

The Théâtre de la Rose Croix was in general looked upon as one of the small avant-garde theatres devoted to symbolism, though, in fact, it only played Péladan's own works. Each of his first two plays was performed there twice. None of these performances received much attention from theatre critics, and Péladan's own influence was limited in consequence. This is no doubt partly due to a certain pretentiousness in the manner of his personal publicity, which provoked a reaction against him, but seen from a distance he stands out as a dramatist of some stature.

His first play, *Le Fils des Étoiles*, was put on in March 1892 and again in Holy Week 1893. It is described as a "Chaldean pastoral" in three acts, and is the dramatic account of the education and initiation of a poet-shepherd, Oelohil. His life is subordinated to the stars, and in the course of his initiation into the arts and secrets of the priesthood his faith and chastity are tested by the temptation of a courtesan; he remains true to his vocation, however, and finally wins the right to marry the simple Izel, his childhood love. This play is written in *versets* which are almost free verse, though with frequent twelve-syllable and eighteen-syllable lines. The vivid evocation of the idyllic pastoral scene and the description in terms of technical and esoteric references to the Chaldean priesthood are completed by allusions to Christian imagery (the Crucifixion, the baby in the stable) although the action of the play takes place three millennia before Christ.

The second play by Péladan, again concerned with Babylonian civilization, and, indeed, entitled *Babylone*, was performed in April 1893, and again in March 1894, this time in a regular theatre, though still billed under the title of Théâtre de la Rose Croix. The Sâr Mérodack, convinced by a prophecy that his city of Babylon will be destroyed, is moved to new sentiments of pity and love by the love of Samsina, the daughter of a magus. Mérodack the proud warrior finally humbles himself before his conquerors to save Babylon, in accordance with the original prophecy, which is the key to the motivation of the whole play. The words of the prophecy serve as a verbal *Leitmotif*. The idea of redemption and in general the Christianization of a pre-Christian story are attributable to the influence of Wagner.

Péladan's theatre was largely isolated from the rest of the avant-garde, partly no doubt because performances at the Théâtre de la Rose Croix were really a private venture organized entirely by the author himself. Nevertheless they did add to the poets' contribution to the new theatre, and this at a time when many small groups, such as, for instance, the Théâtre des Poètes, had difficulty in finding worth-while verse plays.

In fact, other plays of a religious or mystical character, but less pretentious than these, were performed with somewhat less ceremony in two little theatres already mentioned, the Galerie Vivienne and the Chat Noir. Their contribution to the avant-garde will appear as we look at stylistic innovations involving mime, puppets, and shadow theatre.

In the last decades of the nineteenth century the traditional entertainment of pantomime, derived directly from the *Commedia dell'arte*, enjoyed a considerable vogue not only as a salon amusement but as an independent art form. The art of mime flourished in various forms at different times during the century, but more especially in the variations on the Pierrot, Columbine, and Harlequin theme and according to the tradition established in the 1830's by the Théâtre des Funambules. The incidence of this kind of entertainment on the first avant-garde begins with the founding, in 1888, of the Cercle Funambulesque.

This was an amateur group formed by Eugène and Félix Larcher, devoted to every style of mime, and it soon attracted much attention: many of its spectators saw in it an elegant entertainment in a fresh and unpretentious manner, others perceived a source of inspiration from which the literary theatre could clearly profit, a stylization the purpose of which was to tell a story and not merely provide a framework for display of the actor's own personality. The early programmes of the Cercle Funambulesque showed that various styles of mime—the comic, the sentimental, the macabre—might be developed. The fashion spread, and one of the more celebrated examples, *Pierrot Assassin de sa Femme*, was performed by its author, Paul Margueritte, at the Théâtre Libre. Thereafter the programmes of the Cercle are reviewed along with those of other independent and progressive theatre groups, and the contribution of mime to the growth of the art theatres is widely recognized. In a magazine article in 1893, for instance, concerned with assessing the influence of the Cercle Funambulesque, the writer concludes that pantomime, by the very fact of the limitation imposed on the performer, provides a model of the stylization which is needed before theatrical reforms can be successful. "La pantomime sérieuse, œuvre d'art, doit être une peinture de la vie, hiératisée."[6] In a modernized form it may thus contribute to the "total drama" envisaged for the future.

In 1892 the periodical *La Plume* devoted an entire issue to the subject of mime. It surveys the history of the *genre*, and the anecdotic aspects of the founding of the Cercle Funambulesque are described in some detail—from its first, amateurish beginnings to the point where the support of celebrated literary figures ensured its success, and its performances at the Théâtre d'Application persuaded regular theatre managers to resurrect the *mimodrame*. The most interesting parts of this special number of *La Plume* are in a series of articles considering the application of mime to different *genres*—opera, dramatic tragedy, and comedy. These set out to

prouver à ceux pour lesquels la pantomime est une bagatelle, amusement frivole de vains esprits, . . . que les meilleurs esprits de l'époque se sont fait de ce fétu une arme quand il s'agissait de combattre les monstres de l'époque littéraire, tragédie, vaudeville, opéra.[7]

Pantomime is presented as the ideal complement of music in the elaboration of "the music drama of the future". It is seen as the opposite of traditional tragedy, being essentially action and gesture, whereas tragedy in its conventional form is essentially composed of informative speech and appeals to the ear, not to the eye. The lessons which the comic theatre may learn from mime lie in the observation that gesture may be as expressive as speech, and that the brilliant dialogue of much modern comedy conceals a banal or unconvincing action. When a mime was presented in a regular Paris theatre,

> Le public, en retrouvant la pantomime sur la scène des Bouffes, a été surpris; il rencontrait des artistes qui, quoique muets et représentant des symboles, donnaient une impression plus puissante de la réalité et produisaient par conséquent une émotion beaucoup plus intense que les comédiens aux vibrations étudiées.[7]

The evident virtues of pantomime as a dramatic form led the writers of such articles to suggest a possible *genre intermédiaire*. This calls to mind attempts by Maeterlinck and later writers to develop a "theatre of silence"; but fashions changed, and it was not proved that a stylization of this kind was viable. The true function of the Cercle Funambulesque was rather the brief, temporary one of assisting in the destruction of outmoded styles of acting and thereby adding to the freedom of the dramatist to create new forms.

When the first puppet plays were performed, in May 1888, in the Petit Théâtre de la Galerie Vivienne they were received with enthusiasm by a number of reviewers. It may seem strange that observers should see in a puppet theatre the potential revitalizing force of dramatic forms. But the critic of the *Revue d'Art Dramatique* is not alone in his opinion when he suggests that, with certain improvements, which may provoke alterations in the regular theatres, "we are able to foresee, with a little help from the imagination, a whole new theatrical era".[8] Commentators found in the very successful marionnette performances at the Galerie Vivienne a satisfying change from the entertainment offered by human actors, and several of them developed the idea of the puppet as an instrument for a strikingly stylized dramatic expression. The appeal of this extreme of stylization was apparent

to the founders of the Petit Théâtre; and a brochure prepared by
Paul Margueritte to introduce the Theatre to the Paris public
explains the particular attraction of puppets, and at the same time
helps us to understand how this secondary *genre* came to be taken
so seriously. Margueritte first quotes Anatole France: "Les
acteurs me gâtent la comédie . . . Leur personne efface l'œuvre
qu'ils représentent." [9] He adds his own view:

> Tandis que le nom et le visage trop connu d'un comédien de
> chair et d'os imposent au public une obsession qui rend impos-
> sible ou très difficile l'illusion, les fantoches impersonnels, êtres
> de bois et de carton, possèdent une vie falote et mystérieuse.
> Leur allure de vérité surprend, inquiète. Dans leurs gestes essen-
> tiels tient l'expression complète des sentiments humains. [9]

In the Galerie Vivienne, an arcade of shops off the rue Vivienne,
a tiny theatre had been formed in 1886, its first productions being
mainly intended for an audience of children. It was being used for
entertainments of many kinds when the marionette theatre group
of Henri Signoret first performed there in 1888, and continued to
be so used. From time to time there were meetings of amateur
dramatic societies, lectures, performances by illusionists, and
every other amusement. No doubt some of the audience regarded
the annual performances of Signoret's puppets as part of such
amusements, but others discerned a significant and original
quality that was to contribute to the revolution taking place in the
theatre. Sarcey himself, the leading traditionalist critic, looking
back on the marionettes of the Petit Théâtre, apostrophized them
in enthusiastic terms: "votre souvenir restera [ô petites marion-
nettes], et qui voudra traiter de l'histoire dramatique de ces
dernières années ne pourra vous passer sous silence". [10]

The first plays presented in the puppet theatre were adaptations
of Cervantes, Aristophanes, and a version by Maurice Bouchor of
Shakespeare's *The Tempest*. These were followed, in November
and December 1889, by Bouchor's first play of his own, *Tobie*, a
"Biblical legend in verse in five tableaux". The originality and
charm of this simple story made a considerable impact on its first
audiences. Thus, for instance, the reviewer of *La Plume*:

> *Tobie et son Poisson*—légende biblique un peu modernisée par
> Maurice Bouchor. C'est l'histoire charmante du jeune Tobie

allant conquérir sa femme, Sara Ragouël, sous la garde mysté-
rieuse de l'archange Raphaël, qui sauve l'enfant des périls de la
route et lui indique le moyen de rendre la vue à son père.—De
belles naïvetés . . . C'est une hardiesse dont nous félicitons
Maurice Bouchor et qui engagera tout "amoureux d'art" à lire
la brochure de sa très vivante petite pièce.[11]

Bouchor himself was prompted to write in *Art et Critique* of his
reasons for presenting *Tobie* in a puppet theatre:

> Il est bien certain que jamais, au grand jamais, un acteur, le plus
> grand fût-il, ne saurait rendre avec autant de simplicité et de
> force ces scènes mystiques et gauloises du plus piquant effet.
> Avec les comédiens il faut se renfermer dans un genre connu, se
> borner aux types classés; plus une seule petite place pour la
> fantaisie! Et Dieu sait si une légende biblique en vers se prête à
> l'imagination.[12]

The popular element of the work owes much to the influence of
the Mystery-play tradition: the sympathetic characters establish a
complicity between themselves and the audience by explaining
the action; the development is based on the simple psychology of
trial and reward; the conflict may be seen in terms of a rudimentary Manichaeism, with the struggle between benevolent magic
and a pantomime devil; the most frequent element of the versifi-
cation is the rhyming couplet of alexandrines, but some scenes
are written in a variety of verse forms. Altogether this is perhaps
the best of Bouchor's Mysteries, although there is some danger
of the end's being submerged in a rather cloying felicity, when
rewards and punishments are meted out according to the best
traditions.

The next production took place a year later, in November and
December 1890, and features *Noël, ou le Mystère de la Nativité*. The
marionette group had been preparing it for several months, after
the warm welcome that *Tobie* had received, and as early as April a
note in *Art et Critique*, announcing these preparations, concluded
with the revealing comment: "The only theatre doing anything
artistic just has to be a theatre of marionettes!"[13] *Noël* is a similar
series of verse tableaux, in mixed twelve-, eight-, and six-syllable
lines, which tells the traditional story, after an explanatory prologue in which the audience's indulgence is solicited for the limitations of the puppet actors and for such unexpected features as

the conversation between the animals in the stable. The pious characters are presented in contrast to a comic peasant whose first thought is to satisfy his gluttonous appetite. A sub-plot concerns the wedding of the shepherdess, Marjolaine. The whole play ends with general rejoicing, tinged with the prospect of sorrow, since Christ is born to die.

On different occasions each of these plays was briefly revived, but the next new production of Maurice Bouchor's works by the Galerie Vivienne puppets did not take place until February 1892. Along with two unremarkable comedies the marionettes presented a further religious play, with a somewhat more adult subject, *La Légende de Sainte Cécile*. Here Bouchor reproduces some of the popular elements of his earlier Mystery plays, with a conflict between the simple, pious character and the vulgar, gluttonous heathen, and with the same introductory apology, which with mock preciosity takes the audience into the author's confidence over such details as puppet strings and similar embarrassments. This direct, fresh approach establishes the indispensable link between the audience and players. But the play develops into a more complex, intellectual version of religious fervour, nearer to the sentiment of the later *Mystères d'Éleusis* than to *Tobie* and *Noël*. Cécile, the young Christian, converts her non-Christian lover, Valérien, and the two prepare to die together as an act of faith at the hands of Gaymas, who is the typical king's henchman of the medieval play in which farce and piety are combined. The chaste lovers die, in spite of the pagan king's having been carried off to hell, their death wish satisfied in a scene redolent of the erotic and masochistic elements of religious fervour. Cécile is beatified against a background of heavenly choirs. The tone of this play is obviously very different from that of the earlier ones, and it is clear why some critics found it too much for puppets to convey.

Nevertheless there are simple original elements common to all of Bouchor's plays, in particular the opposition between the pious characters and the vulgar glutton whom Bouchor himself describes and justifies in the preface to his *Éleusis*:

se plaisant à étaler sa goinfrerie et sa paillardise . . . Si j'ai plusieurs fois remanié ce type, c'est d'abord qu'il me plaît par la perfection de son égoïsme; c'est ensuite que la nature de son comique me paraît bien convenir à un théâtre de marionnettes

. . . Ce personnage est devenu pour moi une façon de signature.[14]

In the same month of February 1892 two more slight plays by Bouchor were performed, together with a short work by another member of the group, one Amédée Pigeon. On several occasions Bouchor's plays were revived, and their popularity was all the more remarkable in view of the limitations of the tiny theatre in which they were played. The advantage enjoyed by the Galerie Vivienne group was precisely this: their theatre never represented any serious challenge to regular concerns, and their unpretentious experiments could therefore be carried on undisturbed. With this independence, and until Bouchor's ideas grew too vast for their framework, the marionette group was able significantly to extend the possibilities of the theatre—an essential function of the avant-garde.

It is only if one takes into account the widespread dissatisfaction with the situation in the theatre, however, that one can appreciate the artistic impact of these puppet performances. This very dissatisfaction was in Maeterlinck's mind when he planned that his first plays should be performed in a marionette theatre. Maeterlinck also hoped to take advantage of the myth-creating function of the impersonal puppet, in which he saw the extreme case of the heightening effect that may be obtained by the mask in drama, to reinforce the impact of his unusual style, in *La Princesse Maleine* and the plays that followed it. The application of the same idea to *Pelléas et Mélisande* is probably the source of a similar apologia of the puppet theatre by Lugné-Poe. In his manifesto for the founding of the Théâtre de l'Œuvre, three months after his production of *Pelléas* with a live cast, Lugné-Poe cites as a possible project for his future theatre the idea of playing not only the Classics but modern plays with marionettes. It is worth mentioning, too, that *Ubu Roi*, a seminal play if ever there was one and in a sense the most influential avant-gardist play of all, though its first public performance was at the Théâtre de l'Œuvre in 1896, was originally performed with puppets by Jarry and his schoolboy friends in 1888.

From the simplicity of Bouchor's first imitations of the style of the medieval Mystery play, therefore, the influence leads to

Maeterlinck's picturesque legends, which Maeterlinck himself saw in terms of puppets. The new dimension of his deceptively simple style demanded an equally simple and unadorned manner of acting, and this new manner was to some extent copied from the sober and elementary gestures of puppet actors. Hence the puppet play, in the same way as the constraining convention of mime, leads eventually to the variety of experiments based on the principle of the mask, all of which have added to the resources of the twentieth-century dramatist.

Some of these developments were, in fact, predicted when the Petit Théâtre was founded, and commentators soon noticed that certain predictions were being realized. When the last performance of the marionette theatre was announced, in early 1894, a writer in *L'Idée Libre* reflects, in concluding his review:

> Et ne convient-il pas, en disant adieu à ces exquises petites créatures, de leur témoigner toute notre gratitude pour la joie qu'elles nous firent éprouver? Du reste ne contenaient-elles pas la forme d'une rénovation totale de notre absurde art dramatique contemporain? N'allaient-elles pas nous donner une conception neuve des prétendues nécessités théâtrales que nos éminents critiques et nos non moins éminents dramaturges s'efforcent de réduire à d'ignobles quiproquos de vaudevilles?[15]

The last performance here mentioned was in January 1894, when the puppets of the Galerie Vivienne moved to the Théâtre d'Application for Maurice Bouchor's last puppet play, *Les Mystères d'Éleusis*, a verse play in five tableaux. Bouchor explains in a preface that his characters have grown too large for the setting of a marionette theatre and that the *Mystères d'Éleusis* is the last play that he intends to write for the marionette group of the Petit Théâtre. Some had already felt, in parts of the *Légende de Sainte Cécile*, that puppets were unsuitable for representing tragic situations or those involving violent passions.

In the *Mystères d'Éleusis*, however, the advantage of puppets over live actors, as Bouchor and his contemporaries saw, was the ease with which they could represent the supernatural, whereas audiences would not seriously or readily attribute supernatural qualities to live players. The story of the Eleusinian mysteries, the abduction of Persephone by Hades and Demeter's plea for Persephone's return to the land of the living, is, as Bouchor explains in his preface, a version of pagan mystical beliefs adapted to suit the author's own ideas on immortality. The descent to hell, in Bouchor's version, is accomplished by Persephone's mother, Demeter, in the company of a number of simple peasants, whose surviving relatives she has already seen in mourning for them. Bouchor's idea is that life after death requires a constant striving towards goodness, not only on the part of the soul in the kingdom of Hades but from those who have attained the mythical, Utopian heaven. Demeter is informed that all the souls in purgatory will be restored to life if she abandons Persephone to the unhappy Hades, but she hesitates to sacrifice her daughter even for this reward, and the arbitration of Zeus is called for. His decision—to allow Persephone to spend half the year on earth and half in the Under-world—is accompanied by the restoration of the peasants, so that the living learn of the happiness awaiting them after death. This curious story, highly original for the theatre of the 1890's, is told with verve and vigour and with an unusual blend of reverence and familiarity found also in Claudel. It is built round a more intel-lectually inspired piety than that which prompted the earlier plays, given at the Galerie Vivienne, and marks the end of the develop-ment of Bouchor's religious ideas. Until his death in 1929 he con-tinued to publish numerous volumes of plays, mainly based on fairy-tales and intended for children, but also including, in 1900, a version of the life of Joan of Arc.

Another source of the "new conceptions" to which the *Idée Libre* reviewer above refers is the Théâtre du Chat Noir. It may at first sight seem surprising to find, in the introduction to Thalasso's history of the Théâtre Libre, that the Chat Noir cabaret is cited as a precursor of the movement stemming from Antoine. The direct influence of the Chat Noir is perhaps tenu-ous, but Thalasso is right in suggesting that the particular manner popularized by the Chat Noir helped to change the ideas of a public too easily content with what it was given:

> Pour insignifiante qu'ait pu être l'influence du *Chat Noir* sur les destinées du Théâtre Libre, il n'en est pas moins vrai que le 'clan' de la rue Victor Massé exerça une pression sérieuse sur le mouvement du théâtre contemporain. . . . Le célèbre cabaret du *Gentilhomme Rodolphe Salis* a été le berceau d'un genre qui, très

en vogue aujourd'hui, compte déjà plus d'un chef-d'œuvre: le genre *parisien,*—léger, sceptique, blagueur, bon enfant.[16]

The salutary scepticism of the Chat Noir was particularly evident in its most popular form of entertainment, the programmes of topical songs in the tradition of the *chansonniers.* Jules Lemaître wrote, of this café-cum-artists' club which Salis turned into a popular meeting-place:

> Il a vulgarisé, mis à la portée de l'oie [symbol of the bourgeois], une partie du travail qui s'accomplissait dans les demi-ténèbres des Revues jeunes. Il a été le premier à discréditer le naturalisme morose, en le poussant à la charge. Il a, je ne dis point inventé, . . . mais rajeuni et propagé le naturalisme macabre et farce par les chansons de Jouy et d'Aristide Bruant.[17]

In fact, it was under the later management of Bruant, perhaps the most famous of all *chansonniers* of his time, that the Chat Noir became the Mirliton. Describing how the Chat Noir also propagated a mild form of idealism, Lemaître adds:

> Il tenait à l'opinion du *Temps* et du *Journal des Débats.* Son idéalisme n'a jamais 'coupé' ni dans la Rose Croix ni dans la poésie symboliste. Il a raillé celle-ci comme il avait décrié d'abord le naturalisme de Médan.[17]

But popular songs were not the only form of entertainment offered at the Chat Noir. Another successful and popular feature was a series of performances of different plays in a tiny 'shadow theatre'. Antoine, for one, was most impressed:

> Salis, . . . n'ayant pu réaliser son premier projet avec des acteurs sur le trop petit théâtre du premier étage, . . . y a installé une sorte de Guignol. Sur un écran de toile blanche, Henri Rivière a créé des pièces d'ombres chinoises, qui sont des merveilles.[18]

These irregular and unusual performances benefited from the same kind of indulgence as those of the Galerie Vivienne, in that the managers of regular theatres did not, of course, take them seriously; and this independence gave welcome scope for experiment.

The plays performed in the shadow theatre represent an interesting development in the history of the stage, but are less significant as literature. One or two, however, are worth noting, particularly those that confirm the trend, mentioned earlier in this chapter, towards a revival of interest in religious drama. In one of the first programmes recorded after the shadow theatre was set up, in 1888, there appears a version of the *Tentation de Saint Antoine*, possibly inspired by Flaubert's version of the story, and later programmes include a "mystical legend", *Sainte Geneviève de Paris*.

The most celebrated Chat Noir production, first seen in January 1890 and several times revived, was entitled *La Marche à l'Étoile*. This was a Nativity play, composed of a series of images and tableaux by Henri Rivière, to the accompaniment of a text set to music, in the form of an oratorio, performed by its composer and author, Georges Fragerolles. The conditions of these performances clearly required that the text should be subordinated to the series of projected silhouettes, and this seems to have been achieved with a fair measure of success, to judge from the reviews:

> La *Marche à l'Étoile*, remarquable composition de M. Henri Rivière. L'Étoile guide le Monde vers la crèche de Bethléem; et passent les bergers, les armées, le peuple, les esclaves, les femmes, les mages, les pécheurs. Apothéose: le Golgotha . . . Après, l'impression qui vous reste de ces ombres minuscules est une singulière impression de grandeur: même, l'opposition est étrange des moyens employés et de la sensation produite.[19]

A later interesting experiment was the production of a work by Edmond Haraucourt, whose Passion play has already been described. This was his *Héro et Léandre*, seen in late 1893, which is classified as a "dramatic poem", though its poetry is hardly comparable to that of *La Passion*. But the dramatic impression it created was no doubt heightened by the curious artistic presentation it was given at the Chat Noir theatre.

Other, minor authors were launched by the Chat Noir, among these Maurice Donnay, who later acquired a reputation in the field of the comedy of manners. In general, however, the limited influence of the Chat Noir, never more than a subsidiary dramatic activity, was largely restricted to popularizing an unusual and original form, and thereby liberating the dramatic imagination.

In his remarks on the Théâtre du Chat Noir quoted above, the critic Jules Lemaître, one of the most acute observers of the

cultural scene in the 1890's, spoke of the work being done by the
"young Reviews". He was right to stress their importance in this
connection, and, indeed, much of the material in this chapter, on
mime, puppet plays, and the like, and in other parts of this book
came from the kind of reviews and magazines of the period to
which Lemaître was referring. One other aspect of their contribution to the new theatre movement must still be mentioned:
that concerning theories and speculations as to the theatre of the
future.

A feature of many reviews during the period of the birth of the
avant-garde is the number of articles purporting to describe an
ideal form of the drama. Once the breach is perceptible in the
façade of the traditional theatre young writers seem to feel
obliged to commit to print their views on the future theatre, and
tell us about either the form which will surely triumph or that
which all progressive dramatists are urged to adopt. Most of these
pronouncements are coloured by the naturalist or symbolist
sympathies of their authors, or present a more or less personal
version of particular literary theories. Some express an ideal which
in certain respects has since been realized: for instance, the popular theatre rather vaguely envisaged in *L'Art Social* has come a big
step nearer to reality with the advent in the last two decades of the
Centres Dramatiques Nationaux and the Maisons de la Culture. All
stem from the same reforming urge that constitutes the initial
impulse of avant-gardism. It is natural, therefore, that this by-
product of the new and enthusiastic dramatic movement is to be
found in the reviews that serve as the movement's forum.

A few examples give some idea of the range and variety of these
theories. In the *Essais d'Art Libre* in 1892 we find an article by
P.-N. Roinard, the author of the *Song of Songs* adaptation seen at
the Théâtre d'Art, which describes his ideas for a *néo-dramaturgie*
of epic pretensions, and dismisses most existing theatre.[20] The
following year the same magazine includes a piece entitled "Pour
le Beau", which develops the lesson of harmony in the different
elements of staging, leading to a harmonious appeal to all the
senses.[21] In *La Plume* François Coulon, who is a frequent contributor of theoretical articles, writes on "action in the symbolic
play", revealing a surprisingly naïve view in his attempt to solve
the problems raised by new dramatic discoveries; his plans amount

to nothing more than the elementary precepts of dramatic crafts-manship.[22] In later articles, however, he expounds more original ideas, and, writing in *L'Ermitage* in 1893, offers the principles of "ideo-realism" (something combining the qualities of both schools), as the great hope of the new theatre and the major fear of established dramatists:

> Les théories nouvelles sont-elles si redoutables, et leur triomphe déterminerait-il la ruine du théâtre actuellement en faveur? L'Inquiétude de ceux qui défendent les abords de la scène, et les perpétuelles accusations d'incohérence qu'ils prononcent contre nos poètes, quand ils daignent en parler, le laisserait supposer.[22]

In the 1894 *Revue Jeune* Gaston Salandri, hitherto associated through his plays with the *réalisme rosse* manner, explains his new conviction that depressing realism is no longer able to attract an interested audience, and that a new impulse can be given to the theatre by importing a religious bias. This will carry in it the promise of future happiness that is a characteristic element not only of Christianity, which Salandri considers is exhausted, but also of the socialist and the anarchic ideals:

> Ce que l'humanité réclame, ce n'est donc pas un analyste de plus qui la trouble, la déconcerte et la décourage, c'est un chef religieux qui la conduise, par un chemin un peu fleuri, vers ses destinées futures, pleines de mystère.[23]

Salandri's article is followed by a similar disclaimer from Henri Amic, whose realist plays were performed by the amateur group Les Escholiers. He demonstrates that the naked truth is unac-ceptable in the theatre, quoting Maupassant's observation to him that "truth is not artistic". Amic not only demands *vraisemblance* or credibility, rather than strict truth, but aspires also to a vague ideal, insight into which is denied the naturalists.[24]

Other plans are based on the principle of eclecticism. The "new Theatre", described in *L'Ermitage* for November 1893, is to com-bine works of every shade of naturalist and symbolist tendency, and quotes a surprisingly assorted list of thirty-six young play-wrights to prove it.[25] In the same number is another article on the project, "Le Théâtre que nous voulons", which proposes to in-quire into the dramatic opinions of young writers. This provokes a public discussion, mentioned in various reviews, and a reply appears in February 1894, together with a number of enthusiastic letters and a great variety of suggestions for the new eclectic theatre. The practical effect of all these fine plans is soon dismissed, however, in a cynical observation by Maurice Barrès, quoted by the *Ermitage* reviewer: "Comme le dit cruellement M. Barrès, gardons précieusement notre beau projet *en projet*, de peur de le salir à l'expérience."[26]

It is easy to dismiss the youthful enthusiasm and speculation as juvenile and impractical, and, of course, much of it is. But it is none the less an essential part of the necessary process of renovation, in which groups like the Théâtre Libre and the Théâtre d'Art may have made the most impact, but which also involved many others.

Notes

1   *Art et Critique*, II (1890), p. 210.
2   E. Noël and E. Stoullig, *Les Annales du Théâtre et de la Musique*, Charpentier-Fasquelle, 1892, p. 446.
    "The passion described in elegant verse."
3   J. Ernest-Charles, *Le Théâtre des Poètes 1850–1910*, Ollendorff, 1910, p. 219.
    "an unctuousness quite in the manner of Renan, and a sentimentality which is even more modern. He [Jesus] has the caressing rhetoric of the elegant priest of a fashionable parish who has meditated on the drawing-room poets."
4   E. Haraucourt, *La Passion*, Charpentier, 1890, p. 40.
    "*Jesus, leading Peter through the open door:*
                        Come see,
Peter, the pink of the mountains shimmering in the gold of the evening:
A violet shadow is lulling the calm valleys to sleep . . .
Peter: I see.   *Jesus*:
             Before the dawn has awakened the palms
And another sun has risen on the horizon
Thou shalt deny me three times."
5   L. Dumur, in 1899, quoted by D. Knowles, *La Réaction idéaliste au Théâtre depuis 1890*, Droz, 1934, p. 108.
    "Making due allowances all round, and with a slight pinkish

tinge of ridicule, like the whole of the movement itself (it is already a great honour to have provoked something), they will remain as the *Cid* of this pseudo-school."

6 *L'Ermitage*, 1893, Vol. II, p. 120.
"Serious mime, being a work of art, should be a painting of life, with hieratic qualities."

7 *La Plume*, IV (1892), No. 82, 15/9/92, p. 394, p. 395.
"to prove to those for whom mime is a bagatelle, a frivolous amusement for empty minds, . . . that the best minds of the age have turned this mere trifle into a weapon when it was a question of fighting the monsters of the literary age, tragedy, vaudeville, and opera."
"The audience, on rediscovering mime on the stage of the Bouffes, was surprised: it met artists who, although mute and representing symbols, gave a more powerful impression of reality and produced therefore a much more intense emotion than actors with their studied vibrations."

8 *Revue d'Art Dramatique*, XVI (1889), p. 362.

9 P. Margueritte, *Le Petit Théâtre* (*Théâtre de Marionnettes*), Librairie Illustrée, 1888, pp. 7–8.
"For me, the actors spoil the play . . . Their person obliterates the work they are performing."
"While the name and the too familiar face of an actor in the flesh impose upon the audience an obsession which makes illusion impossible or very difficult, impersonal puppets, creatures of wood and cardboard, possess a quaint and mysterious life. Their appearance of truth is surprising, worrying. In their essential gestures is contained the complete expression of human feelings."

10 Francisque Sarcey, quoted by A. Aderer, *Le Théâtre à Côté*, Librairies-Imprimeries Réunies, 1894, p. 67.
"the memory of you will remain, little marionettes, and no-one wishing to deal with the history of the drama in the last few years could fail to give you a mention."

11 F. Coulon, *La Plume*, I (1889), No. 17 (15/12/1889), endpapers p. 3.
"*Tobias and his Fish*—Biblical legend, somewhat modernized by Maurice Bouchor. It is the charming story of the young Tobias going off to win his wife, Sara Ragouël, under the mysterious guardianship of the archangel Raphael, who saves the child from the perils of the journey and shows him how to restore his father's sight.—Some fine naïveties . . . This is a bold venture, for which Maurice Bouchor is to be congratulated and which will persuade all 'art-lovers' to read the booklet of his very lively little play."

12   M. Bouchor, *Art et Critique*, I (1889), p. 407.
"It is quite certain that an actor, however great he might be,
would never ever be able to render these scenes of mystery and
broad Gallic humour, of the most piquant effect, with so much
simplicity and force. With live actors one must shut oneself within a known style, confine oneself to standard types; no longer does
one have even the tiniest bit of room for fantasy! And, heaven
knows, a Biblical legend in verse certainly lends itself to the
imagination."

13   *Art et Critique*, II (1890), p. 265.

14   M. Bouchor, *Les Mystères d'Éleusis*, Lecène et Oudin, 1894, p. 22.
"revelling in displaying his gluttony and ribaldry . . . If I have
several times re-used this type, it is first of all because I like him,
for the perfection of his egoism; and then because the nature of
his comic humour seems to me very much suited to a puppet
theatre . . . This character has become for me a kind of signature."

15   *L'Idée Libre*, III (February 1894), p. 92.
"And is it not fitting, as we say goodbye to these exquisite little
creatures, that we should express to them all our gratitude for the
joy which they brought us? Did they not, moreover, contain the
form of a total renovation of our absurd contemporary dramatic
art? Were they not to give us a new conception of the supposed
rules and requirements of the theatre, which our eminent critics
and our no less eminent dramatists are trying to reduce to wretched
vaudeville tricks of mistaken identity?"

16   A. Thalasso, *Le Théâtre Libre*, Mercure de France, 1909, p. 44.
"However insignificant the influence of the *Chat Noir* may have
been on the destinies of the Théâtre Libre, it is none the less true
that the clan from the rue Victor Massé exercised a serious pressure
on the contemporary theatre movement. . . . The famous cabaret of
Gentleman Rodolphe Salis was the cradle of a manner which, very
much in vogue today, can count more than one masterpiece: the
Parisian manner—light, sceptical, joking, good-natured."

17   Jules Lemaître, quoted by R. Dumesnil, *L'Époque réaliste et
naturaliste*, Tallandier, 1945, p. 74.
"It popularized, brought within the grasp of the goose [the bour-
geois], a part of the work which was being accomplished in the
half-shadows of the young Reviews. It was the first to discredit
morose naturalism, by making a caricature of it. It . . . I would not
say invented, but rejuvenated and propagated, macabre and comical
naturalism through the songs of Jouy and of Aristide Bruant."
"It valued the opinion of serious newspapers like *Le Temps* and

the *Journal des Débats*. Its idealism never 'cut across' the Rosicrucians or symbolist poetry. It poked fun at the latter, just as it had decried the naturalism of the Médan school."

18 A. Antoine, "*Mes Souvenirs*", Fayard, 1921, p. 103 (10/6/1888).
    "Salis, . . . not having been able to carry out his initial plan with actors on the stage of the first floor theatre, which was too small, . . . has set up there a sort of Punch and Judy show. On a white screen Henri Rivière has produced plays with shadow figures, which are marvellous."

19 *Revue d'Art Dramatique*, XVII (1890), pp. 131–132.
    "The *Marche à l'Étoile*, a remarkable composition by Monsieur Henri Rivière. The Star guides everyone to the cradle in Bethlehem; shepherds pass by, then armies, the people, slaves, women, magi, sinners. Apotheosis: Golgotha . . . Afterwards, the impression you have of these minute shadows is a singular impression of size: indeed, there is a strange contrast between the means used and the sensation achieved."

20 P.-N. Roinard, *Essais d'Art Libre*, II (1892), pp. 285–291.

21 A. Germain, "Pour le Beau", *Essais d'Art Libre*, III (1893), pp. 88–92.

22 F. Coulon, *La Plume*, IV (1892), pp. 499–500; then in *L'Ermitage*, V (1893), p. 251.
    "Are the new theories so much to be feared? Would their triumph bring about the ruin of the theatre at present in favour? The Anxiety of those who defend the approaches to the stage, and the perpetual accusations of incoherence which they make against our poets, when they deign to mention them, would lead one to suppose so."

23 G. Salandri, "Le Théâtre de l'Avenir—Essai de Théorie religieuse théâtrale", *La Revue Jeune* (*L'Avenir Dramatique*), No. 2 (1894), p. 53.
    "What the human race is asking for is not, therefore, yet another analyst to worry, disconcert, and discourage it; it is a religious leader who will take it, along a somewhat flowery path, towards its future destinies, full of mystery."

24 H. Amic, "Le Théâtre de l'Avenir—La Vérité au théâtre", *La Revue Jeune* (*L'Avenir Dramatique*), No. 3 (1894), pp. 97–106.

25 "Le Théâtre neuf", *L'Ermitage*, VI (1893), p. 184.

26 "Le Théâtre que nous voulons, II", *L'Ermitage*, VII (1894), p. 108.
    "As Monsieur Barrès cruelly remarks, let us keep our fine and precious project *as a project*, for fear of making a mess of it in the course of experience."

IX

NON-PARTISAN THEATRES

IN NOVEMBER 1886 a group of pupils at the Lycée Condorcet decided to form a dramatic society with the original idea of performing new and unknown works. There was a lengthy discussion on the choice of a title for the group, some suggestions including *The Young Club*, *Les Rieurs*, *Les Modernes*, *Les Thélémites*, and *Les Spectres de l'Art*.[1] In December the title *Les Escholiers* was finally chosen, and the pattern of activities largely established. The group met to choose and rehearse plays, and many of the early performances of the Cercle des Escholiers were given in private, with young professional actresses invited to play the women's parts. The most prominent participants at this stage were the first secretary Georges Bourdon, the brothers Thadée and Alexandre Natanson, Alphonse Franck, and Aurélien Lugné (later Lugné-Poe).

The statutes of the society, reproduced in the *Livre d'Or*, published after the First World War (for the Cercle des Escholiers was one group which survived and continued to flourish after the first, pioneering phase of the avant-garde), show that from the start it was anxious to propagate new drama, and it is this that distinguishes it from many less ambitious amateur groups and café clubs of the time:

I. *But de la Société*
Article Premier.—La Société "Les Escholiers", fondée le 11 novembre 1886, a pour objet de réunir des personnes s'intéressant aux manifestations littéraires, dramatiques et artistiques, et de les grouper dans des réunions amicales, des représentations théâtrales ou des concerts, à l'effet, notamment, de jouer des pièces inédites, de mettre en lumière des artistes dramatiques ou lyriques et de faciliter l'accès des théâtres réguliers aux jeunes auteurs en faisant connaître leurs œuvres.[2]

Les Escholiers thus constituted the first avant-garde theatre group to be founded (starting even before Antoine), and this statement of their aims might well stand as the epigraph to all such groups.

The first meeting at which plays were performed (in early March 1887, just before the opening night of the Théâtre Libre) was thus the beginning of a long series of 'private evenings' at which some items were extracted from well-known works (Molière, Hugo, Musset) and the others mainly limited to *saynètes*, or playlets, and insignificant dramatic jokes. The society might well have become just another elegant amusement, with no literary importance, one of several amateur groups like the Cercle Volney, the Cercle Pigalle, or the Cercle Gaulois. But some members had more original ideas, and in May 1888 Les Escholiers gave a public performance which included some new drama. Thereafter the private evenings continued, but there were also occasional public performances, which were often enthusiastically and widely reviewed. In all in their first seven years (to 1894) Les Escholiers gave twenty-seven programmes, about half of them public performances and many of them including new and original plays.

This first public performance was noticed by a score of periodicals, although it produced nothing very remarkable from the literary point of view. The only play of interest was a one-act comedy by Jules de Marthold, *Neiges d'Antan*, written three months earlier. Set in Paris in 1474, it recounts one of the adventures of the poet François Villon, and is written in an imitation of fifteenth-century language. Marthold had had plays performed before this, but his success with Les Escholiers seems to have helped him in the way the statutes envisaged, since in the following year two of his plays were accepted by the national theatre, the Odéon.

The next recorded performance by Les Escholiers, in December 1888, was also public, and consolidated the recent success of Henri Amic, a young dramatist whose later abnegation of naturalism was mentioned at the end of the last chapter (see p. 132). Amic had had a play accepted by the Odéon earlier in the year, and so his play *Une Vengeance*, which Les Escholiers now presented, aroused considerable interest. In a preface the author describes it as a sombre "intimate drama", though it strikes the reader today as a successful variation on the theme of the moral dilemma of the adulterous wife, a theme which this age seems to have found of inexhaustible interest. In a vaguely aristocratic setting (the nearest that most bourgeois drama came to representing the 'noble' heroes of Classical tragedy) Pierre de Sauges prepares to fight a duel with his wife's supposed lover, unknown to her. He succeeds only in wounding the lover, and there follows a scene of reconciliation with his wife. In the second act the wife hesitates to accept the lover's offer to elope with her at the thought of having to leave her son. Nevertheless the lover arrives outside the house, at night, to escort her, and she decides to leave. Thereupon the son discovers the lover, shoots and kills him, having taken him for a prowling thief. Honour is saved. This study of a moral dilemma is more reminiscent of the younger Dumas than it is convincing as naturalist drama, but has qualities deriving from both. It is also a successful experiment in making reality fit into a neat dramatic pattern.

The later Amic was more closely associated with *réalisme rosse*, in spite of his protests. Two of his plays were performed at the Théâtre d'Application, but his most violently realistic play was *Une Mère*, which Les Escholiers presented in 1894. This brief sketch aroused a considerable storm because of its sordid situation and violent language. An old prostitute lies gravely ill, in the presence of her daughter, whom she has degraded and exploited. The daughter takes advantage of her mother's weakness to express all her hate and disgust, but in the midst of the shower of insults the mother expires, unnoticed. When the daughter realizes what has happened her mood changes completely. She is terrified of what she has done—the mother has died with her daughter's cruel words ringing in her ears—and prays for forgiveness over the corpse. That this play, typical of the gratuitously sordid realist manner, should excite violent protests, out of proportion to its real worth, is a confirmation of the reaction against the starker kinds of realism. In 1894 such by now familiar themes were hardly of interest to the avant-gardists, and eventually plays of this kind survived only in the Grand Guignol theatre, founded by the Théâtre Libre author Oscar Métenier. It was in connection with the reception of *Une Mère* that Amic felt himself obliged to write into his article on the future theatre mentioned above (p. 132) a rejection of the more shocking aspects of lower-class realism, while protesting in defence of his own play that it was valid because of its sincerity.

For three years after the success of *Une Vengeance*, until the end of 1891, Les Escholiers continued to function, but produced very little of lasting interest. One exception was a topical review, *Fructidor*, presented to an invited audience, on a 'theatre club' basis, after it had been banned from public performance because of its political allusions. The interest here is not simply in the fact that Les Escholiers were able to put on a play banned elsewhere, but also that one of its three authors was the young Gaston Armand de Caillavet. He was later to form, with Robert de Flers, one of the most popular pairs of writers of *la belle époque*, specializing in fashionable though not memorable comedy. The pattern of this development is typical of many: a writer naturally tends to be of the avant-garde in his youth, and to move or drift into other sectors of literary activity when the avant-garde have found new preoccupations. Those who continue to be avant-gardists over a long period are in the minority. Cocteau seems to have managed it, in spite of his elevation to the ranks of the Académie Française, though one's first reaction to the news that Eugène Ionesco, the great destroyer of shibboleths of the 1950's, had also become an *académicien* was that something had got to give: either Ionesco himself or the Académie would, presumably, never be quite the same again.

In December 1891 things looked up for Les Escholiers: the young actor Lugné-Poe, who had left the group in 1887 and who was now active in all kinds of theatrical pursuits, returned and was appointed producer-director. He proceeded to produce new plays for Les Escholiers until the beginning of 1893, when his enthusiastic plans took him elsewhere. The influence of the future director of the Théâtre de l'Œuvre is at once visible in the programmes of the society, which are almost all public and widely reported. The first of these programmes includes a play by Lugné himself, written in collaboration with his friend Louis Malaquin, *Viardot et Cie.*, which is an unoriginal picture of middle-class life; a slight comedy, *Anachronisme*, in which some critics saw a *parodie aristophanesque*, which aroused hopes of a new style of satire; and a much more substantial play, Gaston Salandri's *Les Vieux*.

Salandri was, of course, already known as a Théâtre Libre author, and his plays (which have already been described at pp. 60–1) also included another which Lugné-Poe produced for Les Escholiers the following year. This was *Monsieur Chaumont*, an unoriginal and facile work, slight compared with *Les Vieux*. The critics praised the players, especially Lugné-Poe himself, but thought the play badly constructed.

Lugné's second programme repeated the success of Salandri's *Les Vieux*, basically a realist play, and included three other one-act plays of some variety, one of which, *La Faux*, by Jules Bois and Gabriel Mourey, was claimed to have some symbolical significance. The Cercle des Escholiers was by no means exclusively associated with the realist manner; but their audience does not seem to have expected to find any profound symbolism in the works they were offered, and in *La Faux* the symbolism was reported to have gone almost unnoticed, though the audience appreciated the play's psychological acuteness. In other words, even though in 1892 the so-called idealist reaction (against realism) was already well under way—the Théâtre d'Art, after all, had opened its doors in 1890—there was still room for the realist approach. Indeed, far from presenting a simple case of action and reaction, the drama of this time, in fact, follows a complex pattern in which realism and idealism coexist, sometimes even in the same play.

For the rest of the season, up to the summer of 1892, Lugné-Poe continued to produce a varied selection of plays, though not all of them deserve to be remembered. In March Les Escholiers assembled in the elegant surroundings of the Pleyel-Wolff concert hall, where the programme included the recitation of a four-act dramatic legend, *Tamara*, the work of a wealthy Russian princess, Madame Tola Dorian. We cannot judge the merits of her play, as it was not published; but her main contribution to the avant-garde was apparently financial. Among other acts of patronage she was associated with the attempt to revive the Théâtre d'Art that eventually led to the founding of the Théâtre de l'Œuvre, and later with the Théâtre de la Rive Gauche. The last programme of the season, in June 1892, included some inconsequential stuff but also one play of substance, *La Famille*, the first play by Adolphe Thalasso.

Thalasso's three-act play was accorded the most enthusiastic praise. The young dramatist, who was later to become the historian of the Théâtre Libre, was at once welcomed as a writer of great promise whose powerful style was taken as a vindication of Jean Jullien's theory of qualified realism, "a slice of life staged with art". The critics claimed to see in Thalasso what the progressive theatre needed: a young author with sufficient self-assurance to impose his style on an intelligent audience. *La Famille* presents the life and background of a lower middle-class Breton family in Paris. In an authentic setting and with convincing dialogue it tells the story of a woman who, having sacrificed her happiness to look after her husband, tortures not only herself but all those round her, from the position of strength that her sacrifice has conferred on her, thus making happiness impossible for anyone else. The initial impression is of a devoted, almost saintly wife, and this gradually develops into that of an unhappy woman determined at whatever cost that her friends and relatives shall pay for her sacrifice. In a subtle and complex plot the past is gradually revealed to the different characters at the same time as it is revealed to the audience. This is an example of an entirely successful adaptation of realism to the stage; the demonic force which finally takes control of the heroine adds a further dimension and produces something more than a mere realistic recounting of events.

Thalasso's second play was seen, in May 1893, in a programme by a minor amateur group, La Rampe. This was one of the more successful of the many amateur societies formed on the growing impetus of the new progressive movement. La Rampe was founded in 1891, and up to 1894 produced half a dozen or so programmes, mostly of previously unperformed plays. These ranged from inconsequential jokes to attempts to reproduce the cynical realism of the Théâtre Libre manner; from vaudeville to light variations on the Pierrot and Columbine theme. It enjoyed some success with a play by Lucien Besnard, *Les Origines*, a photographic representation of the vicissitudes of a *ménage à trois*. Besnard went on to produce more than a dozen successful plays in the first decades of the present century. But La Rampe's big success was with Thalasso's *La Faim*. This is a play built on the naturalist principle of the realistic stage transposition of a *fait divers* or small news item, and aroused interest more as the experimental application of a theory than as a living play. An indictment of society, it is based on newspaper reports of the mass suicide of a penniless and starving family of mother, father, and five children.

Critical reaction to *La Faim* was lively, but divided. *L'Art et la Vie* attacks the tendency to justify a play by its social significance, and classifies *La Faim* as an "essai inavoué 'd'art social' . . . l'art ne saurait avoir pour fin la réforme sociale, étant à lui-même sa propre fin".[3] The second *Revue Jeune* (1894), recalling Thalasso's play, is much more enthusiastic: "c'est le théâtre que nous rêvons tous: plus de convenu, plus de procédé, de la vie, une étude exacte, minutieuse, vivante, du réel et du vrai."[4] But the oddest thing about this experiment in realism—and in contradiction with this opinion—is that it is written in verse.

To return to Les Escholiers, we find a year later, in May 1894, Thalasso's third play, a three-act drama entitled *L'Art*. Both the Cercle des Escholiers and Thalasso himself were by now well enough known for the play to have a full-scale public discussion by the theatre critics. As a realist drama this work is the story of the adventures of an artist in his search for happiness; as a symbolical play it represents the contradictions of life, the clash of opposing aspirations.

A sculptor unhappy in love, Kermogan—again a Breton— explores the world in search of a new life force, something which will enable him to recapture his artistic inspiration. For a time he devotes himself to the upbringing of an adopted son, and trains him as an artist. Love, affection, even honour, are sacrificed to art. When Kermogan learns that his adopted son is in love with his own young wife he renounces all claim to her, after a long mental and moral struggle. The renunciation is finally made, however, in the name of love, not of art; for the son is to find happiness not in his dedication to art, but in life. Art, symbolized by a statue in Kermogan's studio, takes its revenge for this abandonment, for in a quarrel between father and son the statue falls on the young man and kills him. The philosophical overtones of such a play are complex enough for symbolists, Romantics, and realists each to be able to interpret the conclusion in their own way. The opposition of art and life is a challenging idea, deriving from the Romantics yet surprisingly modern in its applications. In the dramatic skill with which Thalasso presents his play there is little originality—the best one can say is that the tirades and theatrical manipulations are adequately handled. The force of *L'Art*, and the source of the admiration of his contemporaries, is in the conviction and sincerity of Thalasso's manner, the feeling that the author wrote the play to satisfy a psychological need.

Les Escholiers could thus fairly claim to have launched Thalasso. But the immediate success of his style, combining elements of realism and symbolism, did not make a professional dramatist out of him. He became a dramatic historian, and, as well as producing the invaluable history of the *Théâtre Libre* (1909), wrote about the theatre in Turkey and in Persia.

Lugné-Poe was thus responsible not only for helping Les Escholiers to launch or consolidate reputations, but also for the fact that by the end of the season in which he took over—*i.e.*, by June 1892—Les Escholiers were recognized by the younger generation as the most successful, artistically speaking, of the amateur dramatic societies. While the Cercle Pigalle and Les Estourneaulx are content with producing diverting *fumistana*, or practical jokery, as *La Plume* calls the topical reviews in which they delighted, Les Escholiers are performing new and original drama. This policy reached its most successful application in December 1892, in the controversial performance of a French translation of Ibsen's play *The Lady from the Sea*. This was the last Les Escholiers programme in which Lugné had a hand. At this time Antoine had already produced two of Ibsen's plays, but since the Paris critics had discovered Ibsen and since *Hedda Gabler* had been seen in a regular theatre, opinions were divided on the Théâtre Libre interpretation. Les Escholiers, in spite of their inadequate cast, provided more material for the controversy. After this performance Jean Jullien concluded that *The Lady from the Sea* was the most intelligible of Ibsen's plays, Jules Lemaître that is was the most abstract. *L'Art Social* cites these views, and also leaps to the defence of Les Escholiers, complaining of the ungenerous criticisms of some reviewers: "Qu'importe l'indigence de la mise en scène . . . si l'on entend le dialogue frémir?"[5] Les Escholiers themselves considered this production one of their major triumphs.

After their success with Ibsen Les Escholiers rested on their laurels: during the whole of 1893 they produced only one play—

and that in private—a comedy, *L'Irrémédiable*, by one Charles
Esquier, which had been banned from public performance by the
Government censor. When *Pelléas et Mélisande* was abandoned on
the advice of Georges Bourdon, Lugné-Poe left the group and
produced Maeterlinck's play on his own initiative, as we shall
see in the chapter on the Théâtre de l'Œuvre. Other rejected pro-
posals included plays by François Coulon, Henri Amic, and the
Belgian Camille Lemonnier. In the first few months of 1894, however, by which time the coexistence of the Théâtre Libre and the
Théâtre de l'Œuvre was a proof of the viability of the avant-garde
theatre, the Cercle des Escholiers resumed their activities. Each of
their three programmes during this period contained something
of note, which in each case has already been described: Amic's
play of stark realism, *Une Mère* (p. 139); *L'Art*, the third play by
Thalasso (p. 143); and finally *L'Engrenage*, by Eugène Brieux (see
p. 66 for a comparison with Maurice Barrès's *Une Journée Parlementaire*).

After the initial period, up to 1894, the amateur society of Les
Escholiers continued its irregular existence, with four or five programmes in most seasons, and with occasional performances that
attracted the critics, but without ever repeating the series of successes of 1892 or 1894. The *Livre d'Or* of the society traces the history of the group until after the Great War. Although the majority
of plays which they produced during the first period show the
influence of realism of a kind, even when Lugné-Poe, the future
apologist of dramatic symbolism, was artistic director, critics
never predominantly associated Les Escholiers with one particular
manner. As an amateur society of irregular habits, they hardly
produced enough plays to illustrate the shifts of literary influences
which occurred in the eight years that saw the birth of avant-
gardism. Many plays presented by the Cercle were no more original than those of most amateur societies, but almost all, after the
first few private meetings, were new; and among the *saynètes* and
other diversions figure a few of the more serious dramatic experiments which contribute in their way to the development of the
new movement which was to revitalize the theatre.

Another non-partisan theatre, but of quite different origins and
intentions, was that known as the Théâtre d'Application. This is

first heard of in 1887, in the pages of the *Revue d'Art Dramatique*. The initial idea, of a new theatre for young actors, was formulated by Charles Bodinier, then secretary-general of the national theatre, the Comédie Française, in a brochure explaining the need, as he saw it, for a Théâtre d'Application. The *Revue* takes up Bodinier's idea, with a reprint of his brochure in February 1887 and a discussion in later numbers accompanied by encouraging letters from prominent dramatists, actors, and critics. Bodinier's original purpose was to make good the lack of any effective dramatic training for young actors, particularly those admitted to the Conservatoire, where the teaching they received had become more and more theoretical, with almost no opportunity for practical 'application' (hence the title of the proposed new theatre). In this form the Théâtre d'Application would scarcely have been relevant to the birth of the avant-garde, but when the Theatre as it was finally formed turned to playing new and unknown works —contrary to its original plan—real progressive drama was at last given some practical encouragement.

Bodinier was aware that no 'little theatres' then existed, in Paris or anywhere else, such that young actors could acquire the necessary experience under expert guidance:

> Dans le passé, les troupes de province, cantonnées dans les principales villes, possédaient la stabilité, l'homogénéité voulues pour donner essor aux jeunes talents; et plus d'une fois, la Comédie Française elle-même consacra, par d'excellents choix, ces renommées départementales . . . A cette même époque, Paris possédait ou voyait s'élever, destinées à l'éducation des jeunes artistes, de nombreuses petites scènes: le théâtre Doyen, détruit en 1834; le théâtre Molière, la scène de la rue de Lancry, la salle Chantereine, le théâtre de la Tour-d'Auvergne [which disappeared in the 1860's], et bien d'autres, d'où devaient sortir plus tard des comédiens exercés. . . . Ces facilités de travail et d'éducation artistique ont malheureusement disparu.[6]

In an article in support of the project Edmond Deschaumes takes up these points in a later issue of *Revue d'Art Dramatique*. He also describes the failure of the Conservatoire itself (attached to the Comédie Française) to provide such facilities, and contends that a considerable share of the blame lies with theatre directors and audiences (Bodinier in his pamphlet was discreet enough not to dwell on this):

> Voyez le Parisien d'aujourd'hui allant au théâtre: . . . il ira entendre, suivant son goût et son humeur, Mme Hading ou Mlle Granier, et il se soucie peu du reste, car il sait que le reste ne compte pas. Les directeurs l'ont amené à comprendre qu'ils jouaient sur une étoile et sur les clous de la mise en scène.[7]

The Conservatoire, he adds, "se borne au rôle de collège dramatique et de serinette à comédiens".[7]

Clearly these necessary reforms, in their original terms, were not sufficient to have any significant effect on the situation of young dramatists, although they were a step in the right direction. Bodinier even included in the original statutes a clause *forbidding* the playing of unperformed works of living authors, presumably to avoid any risk of being accused of competing with established commercial theatres. He did, however, envisage the presentation of many neglected classics, and hoped thus to revive the exhausted repertoire by an injection of virtually new material:

> Ainsi, cette école d'application que nous rêvons de fonder présenterait un double intérêt: la résurrection de toute une littérature injustement oubliée, et l'avènement d'une foule de jeunes talents qui n'attendent, pour se produire, que des circonstances propices.[8]

Bodinier's scheme is thus a fairly modest one, his language very different from the aggressive tone adopted by some of the young reformers we have seen earlier. Indeed, this tone is inclined to be a little condescending, but the intention is sincere enough, if far from revolutionary.

The fact that this project was so favourably received owes much to the sympathetic interest and publicity of *La Revue d'Art Dramatique* and several other periodicals. This led to the granting of a ministerial *arrêté*, enabling the Theatre to be set up under the auspices of the Comédie Française, in a surprisingly short time (in October 1887), and the inauguration of the Théâtre d'Application took place in February 1888, with a programme of extracts from the Classical repertoire of the national theatres.

Soon after its inauguration it became a common practice for the Theatre to be loaned or hired to occasional amateur groups, not only for plays but also lectures and exhibitions. At different times several of the theatre groups already described took advantage of Bodinier's hospitality: Les Escholiers played there on three occasions, while Lugné-Poe was producing for them; the last performance given by Paul Fort's Théâtre d'Art was given there; and it was also used by La Rampe (p. 142). From time to time isolated performances of other plays of interest to the avant-garde were seen at the Théâtre d'Application, often by groups formed for the occasion. They represent, however, only a minor portion of the works seen there, since items from the standard repertory continued to appear, and much of the amateur production was no more than simple entertainment of no literary significance. The critical reaction, in fact, is often one of disappointment, after the hopes raised by the auspicious beginnings of the Théâtre d'Application with its selections from the Classics.

One of the first informal societies to use the Théâtre d'Application was formed by Bodinier himself a year after the Theatre's inauguration, and, to distinguish it from his group of Conservatoire pupils exercising their talents on familiar plays, he called it the Théâtre d'Amateurs. After its first three programmes (March to June 1889) this venture got short shrift from the *Art et Critique* reviewer, solidly behind the Théâtre Libre, who summed it up as follows:

> Les lauriers de M. Antoine portaient ombrage au nouveau directeur [Bodinier]; il créa le Théâtre d'Amateurs, une entreprise au titre peu intéressant, qui n'a donné jusqu'à présent, ni à son directeur ni au public, de bien grandes satisfactions.[9]

The point is that it was not enough that a group should play only previously unperformed works. The particular gifts of Antoine and his connections with a recognizable literary manner gave his venture a character and a shape that many other groups lacked. Similar criticism could be directed against the efforts of the Cercle Dramatique, which made several appearances at the Théâtre d'Application during 1890 and 1891. Their performances consisted entirely of unpublished (or unperformed) plays, and included works by Ernest Daudet and Paul Bonnetain. A later group, Le Masque, after their early excursions into the standard repertoire, gave a similar series of unperformed works from 1891 to 1894. Apart from the inclusion of poetry by Catulle Mendès and Théodore de Banville, Le Masque's only notable event was the presentation of a satirical comedy by Rachilde, *Les Fils d'Adam*, which was not published.

Not everything seen at the Théâtre d'Application was quite so unmemorable or limited in its impact, and, indeed, several plays of interest have already been noticed in earlier chapters. These include Georges de Porto-Riche's *L'Infidèle*, which appeared there in 1890 after it had been withdrawn from the Théâtre Libre. In 1891 and 1892 Dujardin's *Antonia* and Haraucourt's *La Passion* were seen, both part of the new "wave of mysticism". François de Curel, like Porto-Riche before him, used the Théâtre d'Application as a kind of stepping-stone from the avant-garde theatre to acceptance in the commercial theatre; after his first two plays had been seen at the Théâtre Libre his third, a mediocre comedy entitled *L'Invitée*, had an airing there in 1893 before moving to a regular theatre. Oscar Métenier too appeared in a Théâtre d'Application programme on the strength of his Théâtre Libre reputation, but his later fame was in no way comparable with that of either Porto-Riche or Curel. As a final example of the way in which the Théâtre d'Application served a varied range of interests —almost, it seems, *in spite of* Bodinier's original intention—we should not forget the note of originality introduced by Maurice Bouchor's puppets in their version of the *Mystères d'Éleusis*, described earlier (page 127-8).

The Théâtre d'Application, or La Bodinière, as it came to be known familiarly, from the name of its founder, in spite of such occasional contributions to the progress of the avant-garde, was primarily a fashionable centre of artistic activity. Particularly from 1890, when the premises were extended, the revues, light plays, lectures, and art exhibitions attracted an elegant clientele. While the educative aspect of its original purpose was somewhat neglected, La Bodinière amused and delighted fashionable *Tout-Paris*. At the same time, by welcoming amateur groups and providing them with a stage, it performed a considerable, though possibly unwitting, service to the new theatre movement.

There remain a number of minor groups which, though they may never have lived up to their ambitions, deserve a passing mention. One such ephemeral group (for it is, of course, of the nature of the avant-garde to create short-lived ventures) was the Théâtre Éclectique, the significance of which, as implied in its title, lies more in its intentions than in what it achieved. Like other groups before it, it enjoyed the hospitality of the Théâtre d'Application, where its two programmes were presented, both in November 1892. They were organized by Edmond Runé, and seem to have been better handled and produced than many such amateur ventures; the ubiquitous Lugné-Poe had a hand in at least one of them. The play which aroused most interest was the one which concluded the second programme. Entitled L'Élève, by an unknown pair of authors, A. Faure and M. Nour, it was not published, but was described by one critic at the time as "une aimable turpitude en trois actes qui défie toute analyse".[10] It tells the story of the sentimental and sexual initiation of a girl neglected by her parents, her successive encounters with an old tutor, a friend of the family, etc. La Revue Jeune gave it an enthusiastic evaluation, from which one can gather some idea of its impact:

> L'Élève nous a vraiment surpris. La Formule réaliste qui n'est pas la nôtre et que nous croyons condamnée vient de donner là une de ses œuvres les plus fortes. . . . l'histoire de la corruption d'une toute jeune fille, livrée à elle-même . . . avec ce sujet des plus scabreux, pas la moindre pornographie. C'est bien supérieur à du Théâtre Libre. On dirait quant au fond et quant à la forme d'un Becque plus aiguisé, plus concentré encore.[11]

Unfortunately we are unable to judge for ourselves whether this reviewer had really found something "much better than the Théâtre Libre stuff"—though from the plot it is tempting to dismiss it as just a piece of Françoise Sagan avant la lettre—because not enough of his contemporaries believed in the play's merits to enable it to survive. The Théâtre Éclectique too disappeared after this brief success.

There was no shortage, however, of groups ready and anxious to take their place. In the theatrical notes of most 'young' reviews one frequently comes across references to the latest project for forming an independent theatre. Théâtre des Jeunes, Théâtre des Débutants, La Pléiade, Les Planches, Théâtre Social and Théâtre

Socialiste, Théâtre Populaire, and Théâtre des Indépendants: such are some of the titles of would-be reforming or revolutionary enterprises, though in almost every case these particular ones were never more than projects. The original stimulus for such activity dates from the first breach in the façade of the traditional forms of the drama, which can be most conveniently dated from the beginning of the Théâtre Libre. This released the creative energy of large numbers of young writers, which perhaps explains another curious project, perhaps a joke, perhaps not, announced in the pages of *Art et Critique*:

> Les jeunes auteurs dramatiques dont les œuvres n'ont pas été accueillies dans les théâtres de Paris, peuvent déposer leurs manuscrits au Théâtre des Refusés, salle Dicksonn, boulevard des Italiens.[12]

Not all amateur societies and marginal groups existing at this time were wholly devoted to furthering the new theatrical outlook, but some were at least temporarily involved in the new movement. The most obvious case, as we have already seen, was the Cercle des Escholiers. But another example was the rival amateur group, the Cercle des Estourneaulx. (A curious habit of the period was the passion, seen here, for rather fanciful, 'olde worlde' spellings: *estourneaulx* is a pseudo-medieval version of *étourneaux*, literally 'starlings', figuratively 'scatter-brains', and therefore, one supposes, a joke. The same is true of *escholiers* for *écoliers*, 'schoolboys'.) Les Estourneaulx were responsible for producing, as early as May 1887, *Orphée*, by Charles Grandmougin, whose *Le Christ* was seen later at the Théâtre Moderne. In 1888 a Théâtre Indépendant enjoyed a brief success, including in one programme a play by Georges Taylor, who had got into some trouble and notoriety over an adaptation, made without permission, of Flaubert's *Madame Bovary*. The Théâtre X***, at its only performance, in early 1894, gave a play which the censor had banned from public performance the year before, *L'Automne*, by Paul Adam and Gabriel Mourey, a work with a socialist moral which tells of the struggle between an industrialist and his employees on strike. Again in the first months of 1894 we find a group with the typical enough title of Théâtre des Lettres. The content of their programmes is unremarkable, but the announcement of their future aims is a fair and average statement of the function of these little theatres, in this particular case with a didactic bias:

> mettre en lumière, en dehors de toute préoccupation commerciale, sans parti pris d'école, toute œuvre remarquable par sa qualité de style, d'étude, d'observation, d'enseignement.[13]

Minor groups like these are, of course, only the small change of the new theatre movement. Nevertheless their participation is in the long run just as important as that of the widely publicized and relatively successful theatres. The avant-garde is constantly working in the dark, and a certain independence and even privacy is desirable for the elaboration of theatrical experiments which at first may seem outrageous. This amateur fringe, where failure is unimportant and where literary and dramatic theories may evolve freely, is a necessary complement to the more flourishing little theatres.

Notes

1   G. Bourdon, *Les Escholiers—Livre d'Or*, Kapp, 1922–24, Vol. II, p. 108. See also Lugné-Poe, *La Parade, I: Le Sot du Tremplin*, Gallimard, 1930, Chapter III.

2   G. Bourdon, *Les Escholiers—Livre d'Or*, Vol. II, p. 15.
    "I. *Aim of the Society*
    Article One. The 'Les Escholiers' Society, founded on November 11th, 1886, has the aim of gathering together persons interested in literary, dramatic, and artistic activities and arranging for them to meet on a friendly basis, theatrical performances, or concerts, with a view in particular to playing unpublished plays, revealing dramatic or lyric artists, and facilitating access to regular theatres of young authors by making their works better known."

3   *L'Art et la Vie*, II (May–June 1893), p. 254.
    "unacknowledged essay in 'social art' . . . art cannot be used for the purpose of social reform, being its own end in itself."

4   *La Revue Jeune* (*L'Avenir Dramatique*), No. 1 (1894), p. 44.
    "the kind of theatre we all dream of: gone are the conventions, the techniques; life, an exact, detailed, living study, something of reality and of truth."

5 *L'Art Social*, II (January 1893), pp. 21–22.
"What do the shortcomings of the production matter, . . . provided one hears the dialogue quiver with life?"

6 C. Bodinier, "L'Enseignement de la Déclamation dramatique", *Revue d'Art Dramatique*, V (1887), p. 207.
"In the past, provincial companies, established in the main towns, had the necessary stability and homogeneity to allow young talents to develop; and more than once the Comédie Française itself endorsed these local triumphs by excellent choices . . . At that same time Paris had, or saw coming into being, numerous small theatres intended to educate young artistes: the Doyen theatre, destroyed in 1834; the Molière, the Rue de Lancry, the Chantereine, the Theatre of the Tour d'Auvergne [which disappeared in the 1860's], and many more, from which later were to come forth practised actors. . . . These facilities for work and artistic education have unfortunately disappeared."

7 E. Deschaumes, "Le Théâtre d'Application", *Revue d'Art Dramatique*, VI (1887), p. 14, p. 16.
"Look at the Parisian of today going to the theatre: according to his taste and mood, he will go and hear Madame Hading or Mademoiselle Granier, and he cares little about the rest, for he knows that the rest does not count. The managers have made him realize that they were banking on one star and the main attractions of the production."
The Conservatoire "is confined to the role of a drama college and a school for canaries". ("Serinette" is a bird-organ, a device for teaching birds to sing.)

8 C. Bodinier, *Revue d'Art Dramatique*, V (1887), p. 209.
"Thus this school of application, which we would so much like to set up, would be of interest in two ways: the resurrection of a whole literature which has been unjustly forgotten and the coming of a crowd of young talents, who are waiting only for the right circumstances to arise before they appear."

9 *Art et Critique*, I (1889), p. 73.
"The new director [Bodinier] took umbrage at the laurels won by Monsieur Antoine, and formed the Amateurs' Theatre, an enterprise with an uninteresting title, which up to now has not given very much satisfaction either to its director or to the public."

10 *Le Théâtre*, 11/12/1892, p. 5.
"an agreeable piece of depravity in three acts which defies all analysis."

11 *Revue Jeune* (*L'Art et la Vie*), December 1892, p. 252.

"*L'Élève* [*The Pupil*] really surprised us. The realist Formula, which we do not share and which we believe to be doomed, has just given us in this play one of its strongest works. . . . the story of the corruption of a young girl left to her own devices . . . with this subject of a most indelicate nature, not a hint of pornography. It is much better than the Théâtre Libre stuff. Both in content and in form one could describe it as in the manner of Henry Becque, but even sharper and more concentrated."

12   *Art et Critique*, II (1890), p. 328.

"Young dramatists whose works have not been accepted in Parisian theatres may leave their manuscripts at the Theatre of the Rejected, salle Dicksonn, boulevard des Italiens."

13   Quoted by A. Aderer, *Le Théâtre à Côté*, Librairies-Imprimeries Réunies, 1894, p. 106.

"to bring to light, regardless of any commercial consideration, without bias towards any school, all works which are remarkable for their qualities of style, study, observation, or teaching."

X

LUGNÉ-POE,
THE THÉÂTRE DE L'ŒUVRE, AND AFTER

THE FIGURE OF LUGNÉ-POE, like that of Antoine, dominates the first avant-garde. As Aurélien Lugné he appears in 1886 among the founder members of the Cercle des Escholiers, and later assumes the more familiar form of his name by adding that of the American author Edgar Allan Poe. It has been said that Lugné believed himself to be distantly related to Poe; though an equally likely explanation lies in the considerable reputation enjoyed by Poe as a writer. He is probably more highly thought of in France than in the English-speaking world, and was in particular a favourite of the symbolist poets of the end of the nineteenth century. One of Mallarmé's most celebrated poems, "Tel qu'en Lui-même enfin l'éternité le change", is, in fact, a homage to Poe's memory. We have also seen Lugné, in 1889, as an unsuccessful candidate for entry to the Conservatoire and "suspected of avant-gardism" and in the next two or three years as the driving force behind a successful series of amateur productions at the Cercle des Escholiers.

In the spring of 1893 Lugné-Poe planned to produce *Pelléas et Mélisande*, following up an interest of two years previously when he had taken part in a performance of another Maeterlinck play, *L'Intruse*, at the Théâtre d'Art. Having failed to persuade his friends at the Cercle des Escholiers to undertake this production, and having seen the breakdown of attempts to revive the Théâtre d'Art, Lugné finally presented Maeterlinck's play with a cast formed by his own efforts. This performance was to lead to the founding of the Théâtre de l'Œuvre.

The story of the pure, childlike love of the young Pelléas and his brother's wife Mélisande, recounted in the simple yet strange manner of Maeterlinck's dialogue, had been thought unplayable, so far was it removed from all that was familiar in the theatre. The

author's systematic use of the trick of repetition in dialogue, less
obtrusive in this play than in the earlier *Princesse Maleine*, combined
with Lugné's production, predominantly grey, with a simplified,
imprecise décor, created a strange and powerful impression on the
play's first spectators. There were several features which made the
play difficult to present: the intentional universality of characters
and setting, both being deliberately imprecise; the mixture of the
innocence of a fairy-tale with the constantly recurring, symbolical
allusion to a sinister fatality; the systematic indirect expression by
suggestion and symbol. For these reasons Maeterlinck had pic-
tured his works performed by marionettes, fearing that live actors
must inevitably destroy something of their magic, their sinister
charm. It is true that these qualities proved disconcerting to many
spectators, but on the whole *Pelléas et Mélisande* enjoyed a far
better reception than the other major symbolist productions—of
Dujardin or Péladan, for example.[1] A large share of the credit for
this success must surely be due to Lugné-Poe's talents as a producer. Thus Maeterlinck's play marks an important point in the
establishment of the idealist reaction on the stage; as a play it was
virtually superseded by Debussy's operatic adaptation of 1902.

The beginning of the Théâtre de l'Œuvre is also the beginning
of the second phase of avant-gardism. After the success of *Pelléas
et Mélisande* Lugné-Poe decided to form a permanent company
from the start of the following season (1893–94). This company
became the next most important avant-garde theatre after Antoine's, and took over the leading role as theatrical innovator
after the Théâtre Libre ceased to function. Lugné-Poe died in
1940, but the Théâtre de l'Œuvre has continued to exist, though
irregularly, up to the present day.

In its first season the Théâtre de l'Œuvre played more foreign
than French works, and prominent among these were the plays
of Ibsen (*Rosmersholm*, *An Enemy of the People*, and *The Master
Builder*). To these may be added Gerhart Hauptmann's *Lonely
Lives* and plays by Strindberg, Björnson, and Hermann Bang, all
first performances. This series of otherwise excellent presentations
of German and Scandinavian works naturally led to the accusation
of 'septentrionalism', but the truth was that native writers also
needed the inspiration of foreign drama as an example to foster
their own originality. The cult of the Scandinavians may have

been excessive at times, but it was at least a salutary incitement to the younger French dramatists.

The first French play given at L'Œuvre, in February 1894, was a short scene by Rachilde which accompanied Björnson's *Beyond our Powers*. Entitled *L'Araignée de Cristal*, it is a nightmarish dialogue, in the manner of Poe, between a melancholic youth and his mother, describing the young man's hallucinations. An obsessive preoccupation with mirrors, the feeling of asphyxia, the vision of the menacing, monster spider of the title, all combine in the climax to precipitate the son's violent death. Rachilde, who also had a play produced in this same season at the Théâtre de la Rive Gauche (*Le Vendeur de Soleil*, p. 107) appears to have a highly personal, macabre vision of life which owes little to the realist tradition, though her earlier plays at the Théâtre d'Art had leanings towards realism. At the same time it is hard to classify her as an 'idealist'. Her drama seems to be made up of a taste for the psychologically picturesque combined with a desire to shock.

The important play in the next programme was the much discussed three-act drama *L'Image*, by Maurice Beaubourg. This was hailed as an attempt to combine the two normally opposing tendencies of realism and idealism. Set in the world of writers and artists, in which this opposition is particularly relevant, it tells of the idealist Marcel, who is in love not so much with his wife, Jeanne, as with the idealized image of her that his artist's mind has created. He quarrels with his literary realist friends and insults the sycophantic and charlatan critics of their entourage. He is left to his solitary dreams, even by Jeanne, and goes mad. Hallucinated by the ideal vision of his wife, he begs her to return so that he may see her once more. When the real Jeanne does return Marcel tries in vain to find in her his ideal image, and in a frenzied climax strangles her. Beaubourg's originality consisted in the entirely realistic psychological observation of what, in vague terms, may be called an idealistic state of mind; though Marcel's ideal had become a pathological obsession.

During the remainder of this first season of the Théâtre de l'Œuvre, Lugné-Poe's subscribers saw more Scandinavian drama and heard some symbolist poetry—which delighted the initiated —but no French plays of any substance were performed. Thus the first season did not completely reflect the plans announced by

Lugné-Poe in his original manifesto sent to the Press.[2] In place of the poetic drama which was promised, and of which *Pelléas et Mélisande* had been such a striking and original example, the Theatre had played foreign dramatists, stimulating but often prosaic plays. Nevertheless it was at once recognized as an important avant-garde theatre, and became the most prominent one when Antoine abandoned the Théâtre Libre. The subsequent activities of the Théâtre de l'Œuvre contain the material for a study in themselves, and, indeed, the story has been told elsewhere.[3] A large proportion of Lugné-Poe's productions continued to be of Ibsen and of other foreign drama, his tastes ranging far and wide: Otway, Oscar Wilde, Gogol, the Sanskrit tradition of India. In this respect L'Œuvre took over the reputation of the Théâtre d'Art, of being prepared to play anything original or experimental. This principle, applied by a producer of merit and imagination, is the essence of progress through an avant-garde.

The period from 1887 to 1894 in the French theatre is a crossroads, the scene of the clash of several influences. Young writers, fired by the Romantic spirit that is present in every generation, rebelled against the unoriginal drama of their time. The school of naturalist novelists, at that time the most prominent representatives of the realist tendency, proffered theoretical advice, and finally succeeded—through the genius of Antoine—in establishing naturalism for a time as a viable dramatic style. The symbolist poets, and other idealists chiefly under the influence of Wagner, in an attempt, like that of the naturalists, to annex the theatre, revealed a hitherto unsuspected dimension of dramatic expression. To this schematic and over-simplified picture must be added the new primacy of actor-managers, the influx of foreign material, the contribution of writers who belong strictly to neither camp.

By the end of the period a number of little theatres were established, and, more strongly than the theatres themselves, the principle of their experimental function. The Théâtre Libre, as we have seen, disappeared in 1894, though Antoine, on his return from abroad, continued his work at the Théâtre Antoine (which survives today) before becoming director of the Odéon, after the Comédie Française the second State theatre in France. Les Escholiers continued to work as an amateur society. Most of the other theatres examined in these pages either ceased to exist in or before 1894, or survived only for a relatively short time, to be replaced by other irregular and ephemeral groups. The outstanding exception was the Théâtre de l'Œuvre.

The subsequent history of what I have called avant-gardism is the history of the innumerable groups that imitated the example of Antoine, Paul Fort, and Lugné-Poe and of the dramatists they revealed.[4] To pick out a few examples: Lugné-Poe's continuing contributions to drama, one of the highlights being his production in 1912 at the Théâtre de l'Œuvre of the first performance of Claudel's most widely performed play, L'Annonce faite à Marie; the elaboration of Jacques Copeau's troupe, before and after the First World War; Copeau's quest for the "ideal theatre"; the passing on of his prestige to Charles Dullin and Louis Jouvet; the rise of Dullin and Jouvet, together with Gaston Baty and Georges Pitoëff, to the position of authority of the so-called cartel des quatre; the primacy between the Wars of the actor-producer and the influence on dramatists of the pre-existence of the studio- or art-theatres; the revelation not only of Claudel, but of Giraudoux, Cocteau, Anouilh; since the Second World War, the new visions of Beckett, Ionesco, Genet; the function of the Théâtre National Populaire under Jean Vilar; the extraordinary success story of the provincial Centres Dramatiques Nationaux and Troupes Permanentes and the rather more patchy successes of that other product of the Gaullist cultural machine, the Maisons de la Culture—all these developments stem in part from the revolt of young dramatists and their interpreters in the late 1880's and early 1890's. But at the same time it is at once clear how much the theatre world has developed, and in a real sense progressed, since those years.

Between the Wars the situation is recognizably similar to that of the first avant-garde. But with the rise of the cartel, so called because the four actor-managers to which the term refers so completely dominated the Paris theatre, the status and condition of the avant-garde undergoes a subtle change. Paradoxically it is more soundly established—because it is no longer confined to operating on a shoestring—and yet the dividing-line between avant-garde and commercial theatre is now more blurred. The polarity remains, whereby, in extreme terms, as has been suggested earlier, avant-gardism is the opposite of commercial success; but there are innumerable gradations on the scale from the purely artistic or experimental to the purely commercial. Ambiguities arise, the season's success in artistic or progressive terms may be a fashionable or commercial success too. A fate of this kind befell the tiny left-bank Théâtre de la Huchette, which in 1957 opened with a programme of Ionesco plays (*La Cantatrice chauve* and *La Leçon*), thus immediately identifying itself with the then most progressive—indeed, revolutionary—elements in the theatre. At the time of writing La Huchette is *still* playing the *same* Ionesco plays—their literary and dramatic merits remaining undiminished, but the novelty having long since worn off—and looks like doing so indefinitely, bidding fair to break all records for the longest run on the Paris stage and now representing at best a kind of pseudo-avant-garde.

But the period since the Second World War has seen other features which have modified the nature of the avant-garde, as well as the phenomenon of the trio of 'absurd' dramatists, Adamov, Beckett, and Ionesco (originally Russian, Irish, and Romanian respectively, but opting to write in French—a piquant absurdity in itself). Post-War theatre has burst the bonds of Paris and spilled out into what had been the cultural desert of the provinces. The big difference is that there are now a score or so of groups active in every part of France and devoted to experiment and challenge in drama. What is more, they are subsidized—never enough, of course, but subsidized none the less—and accorded official status and recognition as Centres Dramatiques Nationaux and Troupes Permanentes, this status being conferred by another new factor in the situation, the Ministry of Culture. The other major shift of emphasis in the post-War period lies in the search for a wider, more 'popular' theatre audience, begun by Jean Vilar at the Théâtre National Populaire and carried on with varying degrees of success by the decentralized—that is, provincial—theatres. But the avant-garde continues to be recognizable, through its many phases, even while making use for its own ends of the passing fashion or the current source of inspiration. Successive generations have acknowledged their debts to all kinds of influences: the reforms in acting and production of Gordon Craig, Appia, Stanislavsky; the mask, the theatre of the unspoken; Freudian and other psychologies; surrealism; the cinema, and so on. But it is still unmistakably a case of 'them' and 'us', with the battle joined between, on the one hand, the values of commerce and philistinism and, on the other, those of art and adventure.

So the avant-garde has gone through a process of strengthening through constant experiment, and this has found its reward in the growth of a wider, more appreciative audience and in an impact on the regular, commercial theatre. The result is that today the avant-garde theatre is an essential feature of the dramatist's world, and many groups now enjoy something like the prestige and power of a well-established commercial theatre. Whether the further corollary is true—namely, that specific dramatists have been encouraged or influenced by the knowledge that there is every chance of an independent theatre producing their work—is harder to prove; though one thinks of the collaboration of Giraudoux with Louis Jouvet, of Claudel with Jean-Louis Barrault, and of Anouilh with André Barsacq. Again, when Arthur Adamov had finished what was then his latest play, in 1957, he gave it to be produced by Roger Planchon, the point now being that Planchon was working not in Paris at all, but in his Théâtre de la Cité in Villeurbanne, a suburb of Lyon. The play turned out to be *Paolo Paoli*, and the beginning of a new style in Adamov's drama. It was given to Planchon not because there was no Paris theatre available, nor even primarily—if at all—for a pre-Paris trial run, but simply because Adamov was convinced that his friend Planchon, with his progressive-minded company, would do a better job than anyone else, and felt, with perhaps a touch of exaggeration, that the Paris theatre was mostly commercialized beyond redemption.

In spite of the shifts of emphasis, of the material differences between avant-garde theatres then and now, avant-gardism is still substantially the same phenomenon in the present generation as it was in the 1880's and 1890's. If evidence were needed for this assertion, what better than to compare the critical reactions to the first avant-garde, quoted in earlier pages, with the following assessment of a modern Strindberg revival:

Une soirée Strindberg au Théâtre de Poche.
Le nouveau Théâtre de Poche, qui n'est plus dans la boueuse impasse du boulevard Montparnasse, mais sur la pente qui

mène à Montmartre, 65 rue de Rochechouart, à quelques enjambées du Théâtre des Arts; directement sur la rue. Un vestibule-vestiaire-contrôle, et, tout de suite, la salle; un corridor; trois rangs de fauteuils—treize en tout—et une quinzaine de rangs de chaises rouges. Un tout petit plateau, de quatre mètres d'ouverture . . . Bref, la modestie même!
Les directeurs, MM. Cellier et Leproux, nous font remettre un feuillet dactylographié, où ils s'excusent du long retard de leur inauguration, annoncée depuis longtemps; et des tracasseries, des brutalités et des lenteurs des services de sécurité. Ils sont presque au bout de leurs ressources et ne savent même pas s'ils pourront donner plusieurs représentations de ce spectacle. On les a brimés, au lieu de les soutenir, de les câliner . . . Ils méritaient mieux, c'est vrai, les vaillants. Ils ont des projets et un programme saisissants. Et cette première soirée est excellente. D'une qualité rare; émouvante, humaine. Les comédiens sont de premier ordre. Nous avons passé au Théâtre de Poche des heures hautes et pures, vraiment. Telles que nous n'en vivons pas beaucoup dans des théâtres plus prospères . . . Mon article est long; pour un humble et minuscule théâtre, rarement bien servi. Mais je ne le regrette pas. C'est justice.[5]

This was a review by Robert Kemp, then the theatre critic of *Le Monde*, which appeared in 1957, although in every detail it reads as though it were taken from a progressive review of about 1890.

In this sense too the avant-garde is clearly still what it was in its early days, although, even comparing with the situation Robert Kemp described, often enough the interesting developments now take place—and rightly so—not in central Paris but in the provinces, or, more and more, in the growing number of progressive theatres in the outer suburbs of the Paris area.

But the true nature of what is and is not avant-garde is still the subject of much argument. Ionesco, in *Notes et contre-notes*, has several pertinent observations on this question, including the notion that the avant-garde, being a precursor, a kind of 'pre-style' indicating the direction in which things may change, may very well not be recognized for what it is until after the event, when the particular conquest has been achieved and even superseded, that is "lorsque l'avant-garde . . . est devenue arrière-garde; lorsqu'elle aura été rejointe et même dépassée par le reste de la troupe".[6] He offers other illuminating views on the nature of the avant-garde, which echo some of the tentative definitions of my introductory chapter:

> L'homme d'avant-garde est l'opposant vis-à vis d'un système actuel. Il est un critique de ce qui est, le critique du présent,— non pas son apologiste.
>
> ... ce qu'on appelle le théâtre d'avant-garde ou le théâtre nouveau, et qui est comme un théâtre en marge du théâtre officiel ou généralement agréé, est un théâtre semblant avoir par son expression, sa recherche, sa difficulté, une exigence supérieure. [6]

Most of us would probably agree. But where Ionesco is less plausible is when he argues from the notion that avant-garde theatre is by nature unpopular ("Puisque c'est son exigence et sa difficulté qui le caractérisent, il est évident que ... il ne peut être que le théâtre d'une minorité"), [6] and adds the further idea that the avant-garde is untopical (*inactuel*, because it is in opposition to its time—*i.e.*, revolutionary) in order to conclude that by these tokens it is universal, and therefore in a sense Classical!

> le véritable art dit d'avant-garde ou révolutionnaire est celui qui, s'opposant audacieusement à son temps, se révèle comme *inactuel*. En se révélant comme inactuel, il rejoint ce fonds commun universel dont nous avons parlé et, étant universel, il peut être considéré classique. [6]

This kind of nonsense is a good example of the sort of difficulties in which a theatrical genius like Ionesco may find himself when tempted, or when he feels himself compelled, to philosophize in this way which, it seems, is so dear to the French. In current (structuralist) terms, the avant-garde is at the opposite pole from the Establishment: it is new, revolutionary, and in a literary sense Romantic, as opposed to the old, the conventional, the Classical, whatever Ionesco may claim. But then it is dangerous to take his claim at its face value, since so much of his writing may be tongue in cheek ...

To revert for the last time to my main subject, which has served as a pretext for these reflections on the theatre, and at the same time as a model to illustrate the alternative approach afforded by the notion of avant-gardism: it is worth recalling that the theatre movement of the years 1887 to 1894, which has exercised such a capital influence on modern French drama, derives from a more general influence—that of the broad current of Romanticism. It may well be that the true avant-garde, in spite of recent developments in the way of subsidies to experimental theatres, cannot be institutionalized: the subsidy, now essential if a provincial theatre is to survive, may on balance have a stultifying rather than stimulating effect. The director of a Centre Dramatique who stays too long in one town is lucky (or a genius) if he can avoid being swallowed by the Establishment: one sympathizes with Jean Vilar, who in 1963 resigned as director of the Théâtre National Populaire in Paris after twelve highly successful years in the job.

During the years of the first avant-garde it was the small theatres existing precariously on the edge of insolvency that were also the theatres which played almost the only drama dedicated to artistic values. There is no logical connection between these two facts, any more than the fact of starving in a garret is a guarantee that one's poetry or painting will be remembered by posterity. But by this token the avant-gardists partake of the Romantic tradition; moreover, it happened that it was these struggling theatres and their enthusiastic authors that opened the way in France for much of the more considerable dramatic literature of the twentieth century.

Notes

1   For the critics' remarks see especially D. Knowles, *La Réaction Idéaliste au Théâtre depuis 1890*, Droz, 1934, pp. 259–261.

2   In, for example, *La Plume*, V (1893), pp. 379 ff.

3   On the Théâtre de l'Œuvre in general see especially D. Knowles, *La Réaction Idéaliste au Théâtre depuis 1890*; Lugné-Poe's autobiography, *La Parade*, vols. 1–3, Gallimard, 1930–33; Vol. 4, Sagittaire, 1946; and J. Robichez, *Symbolisme au Théâtre, Lugné-Poe et les Débuts de l'Œuvre*, Éditions de l'Arche, 1957.

4   On the leading theatres up to 1930 see particularly A. Veinstein, *Du Théâtre Libre au Théâtre Louis Jouvet: les Théâtres d'Art à travers leur périodique*, Librairie Théâtrale, 1955.

5   R. Kemp, *Le Monde*, 18/12/1957, p. 13.
"A Strindberg evening at the Théâtre de Poche.
"The new Théâtre de Poche, no longer in the muddy cul-de-sac

off the boulevard Montparnasse but on the hill leading to Montmartre, at 65 rue de Rochechouart, a few strides from the Théâtre
des Arts; opening directly out on to the street. An entrance foyer
cum cloakroom cum ticket check, and straight into the theatre
itself; a corridor; three rows of stalls—thirteen seats in all—and
about fifteen rows of ordinary red chairs. A minute stage, about
thirteen feet wide . . . In short, the height of modesty!

"The directors, Messrs Cellier and Leproux, hand out a dupli-
cated sheet apologizing for the long delay in their opening, announced a long time ago; and for the worries, the crudity, and
slowness of the safety arrangements. They are almost at the end of
their resources and do not know even whether they will be able to
give several performances of this programme. They have been
hard done by, instead of being supported, cajoled even . . . In
truth they deserved better, valiant as they are. They have thrilling
plans and programme. And this first evening is excellent. Of a rare
quality; moving, human. The actors are first class. We spent in this
Pocket Theatre a time of exaltation and purity, truly. Of a kind
that we do not find much in more prosperous theatres . . . My
article is a long one; for a modest, tiny theatre, rarely well served.
But I do not regret it. It is no more than it deserves."

6   E. Ionesco, *Notes et contre-notes*, Gallimard, 1962, p. 26, pp. 27–28,
p. 40.

"when the vanguard . . . has become the rearguard; when the rest
of the troops have caught up or even overtaken it".

"The avant-gardist is the opponent of a present system. He is a
critic of that which is, the critic of the present—not its apologist.
. . . what we call the avant-garde theatre or the new theatre, and
which is like a theatre on the fringe of the official or generally
accepted theatre, is a theatre that seems, by its expression, its
searching, its difficulty, to have higher, more exacting standards."

"Because it is characterized by its exacting requirements its difficulty, it is obvious that . . . it can only be the theatre of a minority."

"the true form of so-called avant-garde or revolutionary art is that
which, boldly opposing its age, reveals itself to be *untopical*. By
revealing itself as untopical it becomes part of that universal
common fund which we have mentioned, and, being universal, it
can be considered Classical."

INDEX

Names of theatres and theatre groups are given in small capitals; titles of plays and other works are in italics

Académie Française, 13, 63, 64, 69, 108, 140
Adam, Paul, 151
Adamov, Arthur, 160, 161
Aicard, Jean, 64, 69, 77
Alexis, Paul, 30, 49, 51, 58
Amante du Christ (L'), 53
Amic, Henri, 132, 138–139, 145
Amour brode (L'), 63
Amoureuse (L'), 62
Anachronisme, 140
Ancey, Georges, 49, 51, 54, 59, 60, 61, 69
Annonce faite à Marie (L'), 99, 159
Anouilh, Jean, 11, 159, 161
Antoine, André, 11, 27, 37, 77, 82, 85, 90, 92, 99, 104, 105, 128, 138, 143, 155, 156, 158, 159; and the THÉÂTRE LIBRE, 44–73; biography, 14, 44, 68; influence, 40, 44, 66–67, 70, 148; on acting, 36, 53, 69–70; on production, 50, 53, 54, 76, 129; realism, 10, 12, 35, 45, 49, 74, 80
Antonia, 118, 149
Appia, Adolphe, 160
Araignée de Cristal (L'), 157
Art (L'), 143–144, 145
Assommoir (L'), 29
Augier, Émile, 21, 74, 77, 109, 112
Automne (L'), 151
avant-gardism, 5–6, 9–13, 34–40, 46, 52, 57–58, 62, 75, 106–107, 109–110, 111, 126, 152, 159–164
AVENIR DRAMATIQUE, 80
Aveugles (Les), 96–97

Avortement (L'), 82
Axël, 37, 49, 105–107

Babylone, 120
Baiser (Le), 49, 54
Ballande, Hilarion, 15
Balzac, Honoré de, 19, 27, 59
Bang, Hermann, 156
Banville, Théodore de, 31, 49, 96, 149
Barrault, Jean-Louis, 5, 161
Barrès, Maurice, 65, 66, 68, 69, 133, 145
Barrière, Théodore, 109
Barsacq, André, 161
Bateau ivre (Le), 99
Baty, Gaston, 159
Baudelaire, Charles, 9, 19, 52, 54, 96, 98
Bauer, Henry, 78
Beaubourg, Maurice, 34, 157
Beauvallet, Léon, 15
Beckett, Samuel, 5, 159, 160
Becque, Henry, 30, 74, 78, 150
Belle Hélène (La), 100
Bergerat, Émile, 45, 46–47
Bernhardt, Sara, 24, 117
Besnard, Lucien, 142
Björnson, Björnstjerne, 37, 59, 68, 110, 156, 157
Bodinier, Charles, 146–149
BODINIÈRE (LA), 149
Bois, Jules, 100, 116, 141
Bonnetain, Paul, 28, 50–51, 148
Bornier, Henri de, 31

Boubouroche, 64, 67
Bouchers (*Les*), 52–53
Bouchor, Maurice, 115–116, 123–128, 149
Bouilhet, Louis, 109
Bourdon, Georges, 137, 145, 152 *n.*
Bourget, Paul, 91
Bourseiller, Antoine, 40
Bouton de Rose (*Le*), 29
Brieux, Eugène, 65–66, 68, 145
Brisson, Adolphe, 12
Bruant, Aristide, 129
Bunand, Antonin, 10, 12
Burgraves (*Les*), 21
Busnach, William, 29

Caillavet, Gaston Armand de, 140
Caïn, 91, 117
Cantatrice chauve (*La*), 160
Cantique des Cantiques (*Le*), 98–99, 131
Casserole (*La*), 47, 54–55
Céard, Henri, 30
Centres Dramatiques Nationaux, 131, 159, 160, 164
Cenci (*The*), 93, 96
CERCLE DES ESCHOLIERS, 14, 15, 37, 60–61, 65–66, 80, 132, 137–142, 143–145, 148, 151, 155, 159
CERCLE DES ESTOURNEAULX, 117, 144, 151
CERCLE DRAMATIQUE, 148
CERCLE FUNAMBULESQUE, 51, 120–122
CERCLE GAULOIS, 46, 138
CERCLE PIGALLE, 15, 138, 144
CERCLE VOLNEY, 138
Chabrier, Emmanuel, 49
Chance de Françoise (*La*), 62
chansons de geste, 98, 99
chansonniers, 111, 129
Chapons (*Les*), 64–65
Charlot s'amuse, 50
CHAT NOIR—*see* THÉÂTRE DU CHAT NOIR
Chevalerie Rustique, 53
Chevalier du Passé (*Le*), 118
Chirac, Théodore de, 81–83, 94, 96
Christ (*Le*), 116–117, 151

Ciguë (*La*), 21
CIRQUE D'HIVER, 117
Claudel, Paul, 5, 11, 34, 99, 101, 128, 159, 161
Cloche de Caïn (*La*), 84–85
Cocteau, Jean, 13, 140, 159
COMÉDIE FRANÇAISE, 49, 63, 64, 69, 146, 158
commedia dell'arte, 110, 120
Comte Witold (*Le*), 54
Concile féerique (*Le*), 98
CONSERVATOIRE, 10, 24, 146–147, 148, 155
Conte de Noël, 84–85
Coolus, Romain, 62, 63–64, 68
Copeau, Jacques, 14, 70, 159
Coppée, François, 31
Corbeaux (*Les*), 30
Corneille, 95
Coulon, François, 42 *n.*, 131–132, 145
cours d'amour, 109
Courteline, Georges, 62, 63, 64, 68
Craig, Edward Gordon, 160
Crapule (*La*), 82
Cromwell, 20
Curel, François de, 62–63, 68, 69, 109, 149

Dame aux camélias (*La*), 21
Dans le Guignol, 64
Dante, 99
Darien, Georges, 65
Darzens, Rodolphe, 45, 53, 67, 77
Daudet, Ernest, 148
Debussy, Claude, 156
Descaves, Lucien, 50–51, 65
Deschaumes, Edmond, 146–147
Divagations, 31
Donnay, Maurice, 130
Dorian, Mme Tola, 90, 105, 141
Doumic, René, 22, 108–109, 111–112
Dujardin, Édouard, 80, 116, 118–119, 149, 156
Dullin, Charles, 40, 159
Dumas, Alexandre (jun.), 21, 28, 74, 77, 109, 112, 139
Dumas, Alexandre (sen.), 21, 22, 109

Dumas, Mlle Marie, 15

Échéance (L'), 54, 59–60
École des Veufs (L'), 60
Ehrhard, Auguste, 24–25, 38
Elën, 107
Éleusis—see *Mystères d'Éleusis*
Élève (L'), 150
Empereur (L'), 105, 117
En Famille, 46, 47, 54
Engrenage (L'), 65–66, 145
Envers d'une Sainte (L'), 62–63
Ernest-Charles, J., 72*n.,* 104, 117
ESCHOLIERS—see CERCLE DES ES-
  CHOLIERS
Esquier, Charles, 145
ESTOURNEAULX—*see* CERCLE DES ES-
  TOURNEAULX
Évasion (L'), 49
Ève future (L'), 49

Faillite, Une, 68
Faim (La), 142–143
Famille (La), 141–142
Faure, A., 150
Faux (La), 141
Fèvre, Henry, 69
Fille aux Mains coupées (La), 79, 93–
  94, 97
Fille Élisa (La), 58
Fils d'Adam (Les), 149
Fils des Étoiles (Le), 119
Fin d'Antonia (La), 118
Fin de Lucie Pellegrin (La), 51, 54
Flaireurs (Les), 99–100
Flaubert, Gustave, 19, 27, 130, 151
Flers, Robert de, 140
Fort, Paul, 14, 80, 81, 90, 91, 92, 94,
  100, 104, 105, 148, 159
Fossiles (Les), 63
Fragerolles, Georges, 116, 130
France, Anatole, 123
Franck, Alphonse, 137
François Villon, 91, 97
Frères Zemganno (Les), 58
Fructidor, 140

Gabillard, Paul, 93
GALERIE VIVIENNE—*see* PETIT
  THÉÂTRE DE LA GALERIE VIVIENNE
Gaugin, Paul, 94–95, 96
Genet, Jean, 159
Germain, Louis, 90–91, 97
Germinie Lacerteux, 53
Geste du Roi (La), 98
Ginisty, Paul, 69
Giraudoux, Jean, 5, 159, 161
Gogol, Nicolas, 158
Goncourt, Edmond and Jules de, 30,
  49, 50, 53, 58
GRAND GUIGNOL, 45, 69, 139
Grandmougin, Charles, 80, 91, 105,
  116–117, 151
Gueuse (La), 82
Guiches, Gustave, 51
guignol, 110, 129
Guignon (Le), 94
Guinon, Albert, 75

Haraucourt, Edmond, 116, 117–118,
  130, 149
Hauptmann, Gerhart, 37, 46, 59, 67–
  68, 156
Hennique, Léon, 30, 45, 46, 49, 54,
  76–77
Henriette Maréchal, 30
Héritiers Rabourdin (Les), 29
Hernani, 19, 20
Héro et Léandre, 118, 130
Hugo, Victor, 5, 19, 21, 81, 92, 96,
  105, 138
Huysman, Joris Karl, 30

Ibsen, Henrik, 10, 24, 37–38, 53, 59,
  80, 99, 108–109, 110, 111, 144, 156,
  158
Icres, Fernand, 52–53
idealism, idealist reaction: 14, 31–34,
  35–36, 79, 90–101, 107–111, 141,
  156, 157. *See also* symbolism
Image (L'), 34, 157
Infidèle (L'), 62, 149
Inséparables (Les), 54
Intruse (L'), 96–97, 98, 100, 155

Invitée (*L'*), 149
Ionesco, Eugène, 5, 11, 13, 140, 159, 160, 162–163
Irrémédiable (*L'*), 145

Jacques Bouchard, 64
Jacques Damour, 46
Jarry, Alfred, 126
Journée Parlementaire (*Une*), 65, 66, 68, 145
Jouvet, Louis, 5, 11, 159, 161
Jouy, Jules, 129
JOYEULX (LES), 57
Jullien, Jean, 15, 28–29, 45, 49, 54, 59–60, 61, 69, 77, 78–79, 142, 144

Karagueuz (Turkish theatre), 110
Kèmener, 105
Kemp, Robert, 162

Labiche, Eugène, 23
Labori, Maître Fernand, 82
Laforgue, Jules, 98
Lamartine, Alphonse de, 96
Lapommeraye, Henri de, 47
Larcher, Eugène and Félix, 121
Larochelle, Paul, 68, 92, 105–106, 107
La Salle, Gabriel de, 83, 84
Lavedan, Henri, 50, 51
Le Bargy, Charles, 69–70
Lecomte, Georges, 65, 69
Leçon (*La*), 160
Lefranc, Fernand, 75–76, 80
Légende d' Antonia (*La*), 118
Légende de Sainte Cécile (*La*), 125, 127
Léger, Charles, 104
Lemaître, Frédérick, 24
Lemaître, Jules, 47, 52, 109, 115, 129, 130–131, 144
Lemonnier, Camille, 81, 145
Le Mouël, Eugène, 105
Lepaslier, Séverin, 84
Lerberghe, Charles van, 99–100
Linert, Auguste, 84–85, 86
Loti, Pierre, 91
Lugné-Poe, Aurélien, 10, 14, 90, 92, 96, 99, 150, 159; and LES ESCHO-

LIERS, 60, 61, 80, 137, 140–141, 144–145, 148; and the THÉÂTRE DE L'ŒUVRE, 59, 104, 126, 155–158
Luguet, Marcel, 68

Madame Bovary, 151
Madame la Mort, 94
Madame Sans-Gêne, 22
Madeleine, 30, 54
Maeterlinck, Maurice, 80, 92, 93, 96–98, 99, 100, 122, 126–127, 145, 155–156
Maisons de la Culture, 131, 159
Maître (*Le*), 60
Malaquin, Louis, 140
Mâle (*Un*), 81
Mallarmé, Stéphane, 31–32, 33, 66, 94, 95, 96, 101, 155
Marche à l' Étoile (*La*), 115, 130
Margueritte, Paul, 51, 121, 123
marionnettes, 115, 122–128, 156
Marlowe, 37, 95, 99
Marthold, Jules de, 138
Mascagni, Pietro, 53
MASQUE (LE), 148–149
Maupassant, Guy de, 30, 132
Meilhac, Henry, 39
MEININGER THEATRE, 76
Ménage Brésile (*Le*), 64
Ménage d' Artistes, 65
Mendès, Catulle, 45, 49, 52, 91, 149
Mère (*Une*), 139, 145
Métenier, Oscar, 45, 46, 47, 54–55, 58, 69, 139, 149
Meule (*La*), 65
Milton, 99
mime, 51, 115, 120–122
MIRLITON (LE), 129
Missionnaire (*Le*), 68
Molière, 23, 47, 110, 138
Monsieur Chaumont, 141
Montherlant, Henry de, 5
Moréas, Jean, 95, 96
Moreau, Émile, 22, 49
Morice, Charles, 91, 95, 96
Mort du Duc d'Enghien (*La*), 54, 76
Morte violée (*La*), 82

Mourey, Gabriel, 141, 151
Musset, Alfred de, 19, 95, 138
Mystères d'Éleusis (Les), 125, 127–128, 149
mysticism, 115, 124–126, 127–128, 149

Natanson, Alexandre and Thadée, 137
naturalism, 10, 12, 14, 27–30, 41 *n.*, 45, 48, 49, 52, 53–54, 55, 74, 77–80, 91, 112, 129, 132, 158. *See also* realism
Neiges d'Antan, 138
Nell Horn, 50, 58
Nietzsche, Friedrich, 108
Nion, François de, 101 *n.*
Noces de Sathan (Les), 100–101, 116
Noël, ou le Mystère de la Nativité, 124–125
Nour, M., 150
Nuit Bergamasque (La), 46–47, 54

Offenbach, Jacques, 100
Origines (Les), 142
Orphée, 117, 151
Otway, Thomas, 158

pantomime, 115, 120–122
Paolo Paoli, 161
Parigot, Hippolyte, 22
Parisienne (La), 30
Passion (La), 116, 117–118, 130, 149
Patrie en Danger (La), 53
Péladan, Joséphin, 82, 116, 119–120, 156
Pelléas et Mélisande, 80, 90, 126, 145, 155–156, 158
Pelote (La), 50–51
Père Lebonnard (Le), 64, 77
PETIT THÉÂTRE DE LA GALERIE VIVIENNE, 115–116, 120, 122–127, 128, 129
Petite Bête (La), 91
Pierrot Assassin de sa Femme, 51, 121
Pigeon, Amédée, 126
Pitoëff, Georges, 159

PLÉIADE (LA), 150
Planchon, Roger, 11, 40, 76, 161
PLANCHES (LES), 150
Poe, Edgar Allan, 52, 54, 96, 155, 157
poetic drama, 31–34, 46, 49, 52, 53, 56, 66, 77, 90–101, 104–105
Porto-Riche, Georges de, 62, 63, 68, 149
Princesse Maleine (La), 126, 156
Prose (La), 51–52, 60
Prostituée, 81, 82, 94
Pujo, Maurice, 107–109
puppets, 114, 122–128, 156

Quarts d'Heure (Les), 51
Quillard, Pierre, 66, 79, 93–94, 97

Rachilde, Mme, 66, 92–93, 94, 95–96, 99, 107, 149, 157
Racine, 5
RAMPE (LA), 142–143, 148
Rançon (La), 60–61
realism, 14, 28, 29, 30, 35–36, 41 *n.*, 47, 50, 51, 52, 58, 60–61, 74, 76–78, 80, 141–143, 150, 157; in staging, 36, 50, 52–53, 54, 70, 76–77; 'Théâtre Libre realism', réalisme rosse: 12, 29, 30, 45, 46, 49, 54–55, 64, 69, 81–83, 96, 132, 139, 142, 150. *See also* naturalism
Reconquise, 84
Régnier, Henri de, 95, 96
Reine Fiammette (La), 52
religious drama, 115–120, 123–126, 127–128, 130
Remacle, Adrien, 91
Renan, Ernest, 117
Richepin, Jean, 84
Rimbaud, Arthur, 99
Rivière, Henri, 129, 130
Rod, Édouard, 91
Roinard, Paul-Napoléon, 98–99, 131
ROSE CROIX—*see* THÉÂTRE DE LA ROSE CROIX
Rosny, Honoré and Justin, 50, 58
Runé, Edmond, 150
Rzewuski, Stanislas, 54

Sainte Geneviève de Paris, 130

Salandri, Gaston, 49, 51–52, 59, 60–61, 69, 77, 132, 140–141

Salis, Rodolphe, 128

Samuel, Fernand, 48

Sarcey, Francisque, 22, 24, 47, 76, 123

Sardou, Victorien, 21–22, 24, 28, 49, 77, 109

Saxe-Meiningen, Grand Duke of, 76

Schuré, Édouard, 100

Scribe, Eugène, 20–21, 22, 108–109

Sée, Edmond, 40

Sérénade (La), 59

Shakespeare, 32, 37, 76, 123

Shelley, 93, 95, 96, 99

Shylock, 118

Signoret, Henri, 123

Song of Songs (The), 98–99, 131

Soulier de Satin (Le), 101

Sous-Offs, 50

Stanislavsky, Konstantin, 160

Stendhal, 19

Strindberg, August, 37, 59, 156, 161

symbolism, 14, 27, 31–34, 35, 90, 92, 94, 95, 97, 98–99, 101, 112, 119, 141, 155–156, 157, 158. *See also* idealism

Tamara, 141

Taylor, Georges, 151

Tentation de Saint Antoine (La), 130

Terre (La), 28, 50, 60

Tête d'Or, 99

Thalasso, Adolphe, 70 *n*., 110–111, 128, 141–144, 145

THÉÂTRE—*see also* CERCLE

THÉÂTRE ANTOINE, 158

THÉÂTRE CHANTEREINE, 146

THÉÂTRE D'AMATEURS, 148

THÉÂTRE D'APPLICATION, 39, 62, 63, 78, 110, 117, 118, 121, 127, 139, 145–149, 150

THÉÂTRE D'ART, 14, 15, 31, 36, 39, 56, 66, 79, 80, 81, 90–101, 104, 116, 131, 133, 141, 148, 155, 157, 158

THÉÂTRE D'ART SOCIAL, 76, 80, 83–87

THÉÂTRE DE LA CITÉ, 161

THÉÂTRE DE LA GALERIE VIVIENNE—*see* PETIT THÉÂTRE DE LA GALERIE VIVIENNE

THÉÂTRE DE LA HUCHETTE, 160

THÉÂTRE DE LA RIVE GAUCHE, 92, 105–107, 141, 157

THÉÂTRE DE LA ROSE CROIX, 119–120

THÉÂTRE DE LA RUE DE LANCRY, 146

THÉÂTRE DE LA TOUR D'AUVERGNE, 48, 146

THÉÂTRE DE L'ODÉON, 37, 53, 62, 118, 138, 158

THÉÂTRE DE L'ŒUVRE, 10, 14, 34, 36, 38, 59, 90, 92, 104, 126, 141, 145, 155–158, 159

THÉÂTRE DE POCHE, 161–162

THÉÂTRE DES ARTS, 162

THÉÂTRE DES BOUFFES, 122

THÉÂTRES DES DÉBUTANTS, 150

THÉÂTRE DES FUNAMBULES, 120

THÉÂTRE DES INDÉPENDANTS, 151

THÉÂTRE DES JEUNES, 150

THÉÂTRE DES LETTRES, 151

THÉÂTRE DES POÈTES, 104–105, 117, 120

THÉÂTRE DES REFUSÉS, 151

THÉÂTRE DOYEN, 146

THÉÂTRE DU CHAT NOIR, 15, 116, 118, 120, 128–130

THÉÂTRE DUPREZ, 96

THÉÂTRE DU VAUDEVILLE, 62, 63, 109, 118

THÉÂTRE ÉCLECTIQUE, 150

THÉÂTRE IDÉALISTE, 90–91

THÉÂTRE INDÉPENDANT, 151

THÉÂTRE LIBRE, 10, 11, 14, 15, 29–30, 36, 37, 39, 44–70, 76, 77, 78, 79, 80, 82, 83, 84, 90, 91, 93, 95, 101, 104, 110, 112, 121, 128, 133, 138, 139, 141, 142, 144, 145, 148, 149, 151, 156, 158. *See also* Antoine, André; realism

THÉÂTRE MEININGER, 76

THÉÂTRE MIXTE, 90, 91, 93, 117

THÉÂTRE MODERNE, 80–81, 116–117, 118, 151

THÉÂTRE MOLIÈRE, 146
THÉÂTRE NATIONAL POPULAIRE, 58, 159, 160, 164
THÉÂTRE POPULAIRE, 151
THÉÂTRE RÉALISTE, 80, 81–83
THÉÂTRE SOCIAL, 150
THÉÂTRE SOCIALISTE, 150–151
THÉÂTRE X***, 151
Thérèse Raquin, 29
Tobie, 123–124, 125
Tolstoy, Leo, 37, 49, 67, 108
Troupes Permanentes, 159, 160
Turkish theatre, 110

Ubu Roi, 126

VAUDEVILLE—*see* THÉÂTRE DU VAUDE-
VILLE
Veilleuses (Les), 93
Vendeur de Soleil (Le), 107, 157
Vengeance (Une), 138–139
Vercingétorix, 100

Verlaine, Paul, 91, 94–95, 96
Viardot et Cie., 140
Viélé-Griffin, Francis, 96
Vieux (Les), 61, 140–141
Vilar, Jean, 11, 40, 58, 76, 159, 160, 164
Villiers de l'Isle-Adam, Auguste de, 37, 45, 49, 91, 95, 105–107, 119
Vitu, Auguste, 47
VIVIENNE—*see* PETIT THÉÂTRE DE LA GALERIE VIVIENNE
Voix du Sang (La), 92–93
Voyage de Monsieur Perrichon (Le), 23

Wagner, Richard, 32–33, 34, 37, 98, 100, 101, 118, 119, 120, 158
Wilde, Oscar, 160
Wolff, Albert, 22, 64
Wolff, Pierre, 64–65, 69

Zola, Émile, 27–30, 34, 39, 46, 49, 50, 53–54, 60, 77, 78, 82